Crocheting Novelty Pot Holders

Edited by
Linda Macho

Dover Publications, Inc.
New York

Basic Crochet Stitches

1 . . . Chain (ch): Make a loop on hook, thread over and draw main length of thread through. Continue to draw thread through each new loop for length desired.

2 . . . Single Crochet (s c): Insert hook under 2 loops of st, draw thread through (2 loops on hook), thread over, draw through both loops on hook.

3 . . . Double Crochet (d c): Thread over, insert hook in st and draw thread through (3 loops on hook); thread over, draw through 2 loops, thread over, draw through 2 remaining loops. Work **Half Double Crochet (half d c)** like d c, but draw thread through all 3 loops at once.

4 . . . Treble (tr): Thread over twice, insert hook in st and draw thread through (4 loops on hook); thread over and work off 2 loops at a time as for a d c. For a **Double Treble (d tr)**, thread over 3 times; and for a **Triple Treble (tr tr)**. thread over 4 times, working off 2 loops at a time as in the tr.

5 . . . Slip Stitch (sl st): Insert hook in st, catch thread and, with one motion, draw thread through both the st and the 1 loop on hook.

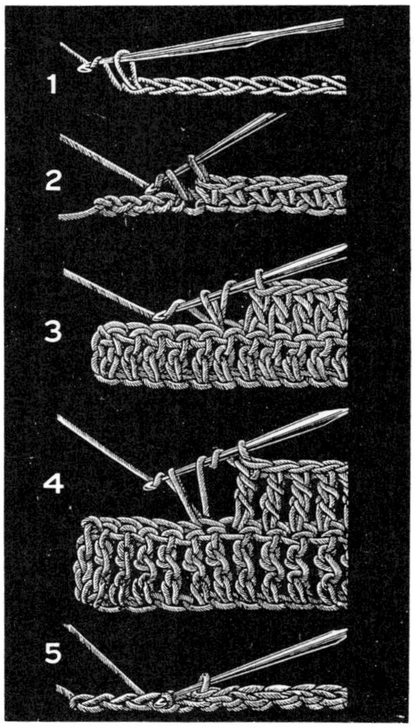

Abbreviations in Crochet

ch	chain	**sk**	skip
sc	single crochet	**sl st**	slip stitch
half dc	half double crochet	**sp**	space
dc	double crochet	**st(s)**	stitch(es)
tr	treble	**rnd**	round
d tr	double treble	**incl**	inclusive
p	picot	**inc**	increase
		dec	decrease

General Instructions

* (asterisk) . . . Repeat the instructions following the asterisk as many more times as specified, in addition to the original.

Repeat instructions in parentheses as many times as specified. For example: **"(Ch 5, sc in next sc) 5 times"** means to make all that is in parentheses 5 times in all.

PADDING . . . Cut flannel or cotton batting slightly smaller, and lining material slightly larger, than crocheted piece. Place padding between crocheted piece and lining. Turn under edges of lining and sew to edges of crocheted piece with neat over-and-over stitches. For pot holders consisting of 2 crocheted pieces, insert padding between crochet and sew up edges.

Published in Canada by General Publishing Company, Ltd., 30 Lesmill Road, Don Mills, Toronto, Ontario.
Published in the United Kingdom by Constable and Company, Ltd., 10 Orange Street, London WC2H 7EG.

This Dover edition, first published in 1982, is a new selection of patterns from *Pot Holders*, Book No. 222, published by The Spool Cotton Company, New York, in 1945; *Star Potholders*, Book No. 55, published by the American Thread Company, New York, in 1947; *Pot Holders*, Book No. 243, published by The Spool Cotton Company in 1948; *Pocket Potholders*, Book No. 69, published by the American Thread Company in 1950; *New Book of Pot Holders and Hot Platter Mats*, Book No. 274, published by The Spool Cotton Company in 1951; *Lily's Sugar 'N Cream Crochet Favorites*, Book No. 62, published by the Lily Mills Company, Shelby, NC, in 1951; *Pot Holders for Kitchen Pick-Me-Ups*, Book No. 294, published by The Spool Cotton Company in 1952; *Pot Holders*, Book No. 101, published by the American Thread Company in 1953; *40 Hot Pot Holders and Other Gadgets*, Book No. 9307, published by The Thread Mills, Inc., Chicago, n.d.; *Lily Pot Holders and Oven Mitts*, Book No. 59, published by the Lily Mills Company, n.d.

Manufactured in the United States of America
Dover Publications, Inc.
180 Varick Street
New York, N.Y. 10014

Library of Congress Cataloging in Publication Data
Main entry under title:

Crocheting novelty pot holders.

1. Crocheting. 2. Pot holders. I. Macho, Linda, 1955-
TT825.C7548 746.9 81-19404
ISBN 0-486-24296-X AACR2

Introduction

Crocheting pot holders is a relaxing, enjoyable activity, and one that can be a welcome diversion from crocheting a more serious project such as a doily, tablecloth or bedspread. What can be more satisfying than crocheting a project that requires a minimal amount of thread, can be completed in an evening or two, and results in an appealing and useful item? There'll be no more burnt fingers if you take time out to whip up a few of these amusing pot holders. Attractive and useful in your own kitchen, they are wonderful little gifts for showers, housewarming or dinner parties, and as inexpensive but personal birthday and holiday presents. In this collection of 64 delightful patterns, you'll be sure to find a pot holder to suit every personality or occasion. Another plus is that many of these projects can be stuffed and used as trivets, pincushions, sachets or toys!

Some of the designs in this book are so simple that they can be used to teach a child to crochet; the distinctive and whimsical motifs are perfectly suited to fire a child's imagination and the projects can be completed quickly to maintain the child's interest. A novice in the art of the crochet hook can learn her first lesson fashioning the *Strawberry* on page 9 or the *Christmas Ornament* on page 47; a master crocheter can work up the more elaborate pot holders such as the *Honeymoon Cottage* on page 41 or the *Hobby Horse* on page 24. But whatever your level of expertise, you'll find many pot holders in this book that will be worth the challenge of crocheting them.

Since the patterns in this book all come from instruction brochures first published over thirty years ago, some of the threads listed with the patterns may no longer be available. Other threads of similar weight may be substituted. If you are having trouble locating a suitable thread, check with your local needlework shop or department and buy thread that is compatible with the recommended hook size; where no hook size is given, use a No. 1 steel crochet hook. Whatever type of thread you decide to use, be certain to buy a sufficient amount of the same dye lot to complete the project; it is often impossible to match shades later because of the variation in dye lots. *Note:* Most of the patterns in this book do not specify gauge; this is because each project is so small and self-contained that the successful outcome of the project does not depend upon the gauge. Each pot holder will vary in size depending upon the type of thread you choose and the tightness (or looseness) of your stitches.

Since these pot holders will be used around fire and heat sources, it is recommended that you crochet with an all-cotton thread and line your pot holders with an all-cotton or wool fabric; do not use synthetic threads or fabrics! At all times, keep the pot holders well out of the way of any flame or heat to prevent damage.

The crochet terminology and hooks listed in this book are those used in the United States. The following charts give the U.S. name of crochet stitches and their equivalents in other countries and the equivalents to U.S. crochet hook sizes. Crocheters should become thoroughly familiar with the differences in both crochet terms and hook sizes before starting any project.

Stitch Conversion Chart

U.S. Name	*Equivalent*
Chain	Chain
Slip	Single crochet
Single crochet	Double crochet
Half-double or short-double crochet	Half-treble crochet
Double crochet	Treble crochet
Treble crochet	Double-treble crochet
Double-treble crochet	Treble-treble crochet
Treble-treble or long-treble crochet	Quadruple-treble crochet
Afghan stitch	Tricot crochet

Hook Conversion Chart

Aluminum

U.S. Size	B	C	D	E	F	G	H	I	J	K
British & Canadian Size	12	11	10	9	8	7	5	4	3	2
Metric Size	2½	3	—	3½	4	4½	5	5½	6	7

Steel

U.S. Size	00	0	1	2	3	4	5	6
British & Canadian Size	000	00	0	1	-	1½	2	2½

Sliced Apple

Shown in color on the back cover.

MATERIALS:

J. & P. Coats "Knit-Cro-Sheen," Art. A.64, 1 ball each of No. 1 White, No. 9 Yellow, No. 126 Spanish Red, No. 48 Hunter's Green and No. 17 Shaded Browns; or

J. & P. Coats or Clark's O.N.T. Pearl Cotton, Art. A. or B.19, Size 5, 2 balls of White; 1 ball each of No. 48 Hunter's Green, No. 126 Spanish Red, No. 43 Dk. Yellow and No. 81 Dk. Brown; and

J. & P. Coats Six Strand Embroidery Floss, Art. A.11, or **Clark's O.N.T. Six Strand Cotton,** Art. B.11, 1 skein of No. 12 Black.

Milwards Steel Crochet Hook No. 7.

A piece of red felt for lining.

Starting at center with Yellow, ch 6. Join with sl st to form ring. **1st rnd:** Ch 3, 15 dc in ring, ch 3, sl st in ring. **2nd rnd:** 5 sc over first ch-3, sc in next 5 dc, 2 sc in each of next 2 dc, 3 sc in next dc, 2 sc in each of next 2 dc, 5 sc over next ch 3, sl st in first sc. **3rd rnd:** Sl st in next sc, sc in next 2 sc, dc in next 11 sc, 3 dc in next sc, dc in next 11 sc, sc in next 2 sc, sl st in next 2 sc. Join with sl st to first sl st. **4th rnd:** Sl st in next sl st, 2 sc in each of next 3 sts, sc in next 11 dc, 3 sc in next dc, sc in next 11 dc, 2 sc in each of next 3 sts, sl st in next 2 sl sts. Join and break off. **5th rnd:** Attach White to first st, ch 3, dc in next 5 sts, 2 dc in each of next 2 sc, dc in next 8 sc, 2 dc in each of next 2 sc, dc in next 5 sc, 2 dc in each of next 2 sc, dc in next 8 sc, 2 dc in each of next 2 sc, dc in next 6 sts. Join to top of ch-3. **6th rnd:** Sc in same place as sl st, sc in next dc, half dc in next 2 dc, dc in next 3 dc, tr in next 3 dc, 2 tr in next dc, 2 dc in each of next 3 dc, dc in next 5 dc, 2 dc in next dc, dc in next 9 dc, 2 dc in next dc, dc in next 5 dc, 2 dc in each of next 3 dc, 2 tr in next dc, tr in next 3 dc, dc in next 3 dc, half dc in next 2 dc, sc in next 2 dc. Join. **7th rnd:** Sc in same place as sl st, sc in next st, half dc in next 2 sts, 2 dc in each of next 2 sts, 2 tr in each of next 2 sts, tr in next 4 sts, (2 dc in each of next 2 sts, dc in next 4 sts) twice; 2 dc in next st, dc in next 9 sts, 2 dc in next st, (dc in next 4 sts, 2 dc in each of next 2 sts) twice; tr in next 4 sts, 2 tr in each of next 2 sts, 2 dc in each of next 2 sts, half dc in next 2 sts, sc in next 2 sts. Join. **8th rnd:** Sc in same place as sl st, sc in next sc, half dc in next 2 sts, 2 dc in each of next 2 sts, 2 tr in each of next 2 sts, tr in next 4 sts, (2 dc in each of next 2 sts, dc in next 4 sts) 3 times; 2 dc in next st, dc in next 15 sts, 2 dc in next st, (dc in next 4 sts, 2 dc in each of next 2 sts) 3 times; tr in next 4 sts, 2 tr in each of next 2 sts, 2 dc in each of next 2 sts, half dc in next 2 sts, sc in next 2 sts. Join. **9th rnd:** Ch 2, half dc in same place as sl st, half dc in next 2 sts, dc in next 3 sts, tr in next 3 sts, 2 tr in each of next 3 sts, tr in next 6 sts, dc in next 15 sts, 2 dc in each of next 2 sts, dc in next 4 sts, 2 dc in next st, dc in next 19 sts, 2 dc in next st, dc in next 4 sts, 2 dc in each of next 2 sts, dc in next 15 sts, tr in next 6 sts, 2 tr in each of next 3 sts, tr in next 3 sts, dc in next 3 sts, half dc in next 3 sts. Join to first half dc. **10th rnd:** Ch 3, dc in next 9 sts, 2 dc in each of next 2 sts, tr in next 25 sts, 2 dc in each of next 2 sts, dc in next 4 sts, 2 dc in next st, dc in next 23 sts, 2 dc in next st, dc in next 4 sts, 2 dc in each of the next 2 sts, tr in next 25 sts, 2 dc in each of next 2 sts, dc in next 10 sts. Join. **11th rnd:** Sc in same place as sl st, sc in each st around. Join and break off. **12th rnd:** Attach Red to same place as sl st, sc in same place, sc in each sc around. Join. **13th rnd:** Sl st in next 3 sc, sc in each sc around to within last 4 sc, sl st in last 4 sc. Join. **14th rnd:** Sl st in next 5 sts, sc in each st around to within last 6 sts, sl st in last 6 sts. Join and break off. Make another piece the same way.

LEAF (Make 2) . . . Starting at center with Green, ch 30. **1st rnd:** Sc in 2nd ch from hook and in next 2 ch, half dc in next 3 ch, dc in next 3 ch, tr in next 3 ch, d tr in next 5 ch, **tr** in next 3 ch, dc in next 3 ch, half dc in next 3 ch, sc in next 2 ch, 3 sc in next ch (tip of leaf); working along opposite side of starting chain make sc in next 2 ch, half dc in next 3 ch, dc in next 3 ch, tr in next 5 ch, dc in next 3 ch, half dc in next 3 ch, 2 sc in same place as first sc. **2nd and 3rd rnds:** Sc in each st around, making 3 sc in center sc of each 3-sc group. Join and break off at end of 3rd rnd. Embroider veins with Black Embroidery Floss.

STEM (Make 2) . . . Starting at long side with Brown, make a chain 3 inches long. **1st row:** Dc in 4th ch from hook and in each ch for 1 inch, 2 dc in each remaining ch (leaving 1 inch free from beginning of row), sl st in next ch on opposite side of starting chain to form loop. Break off.

With Black Embroidery Floss, embroider 2 lazy daisy sts on each side of center for seeds. Cut a piece of felt slightly larger than outer edge of each pot holder piece. Sew in place so felt overlaps edge slightly. Sew stem in place. Sew edge of leaf to each side. Sew loose ends of leaf together. Sew pot holder pieces together at top over rounded sides for 3 inches. ✿

Red Apple

This holder may be made with any of the American Thread Company products listed below:

Material	Quantity	Size of Needle
"STAR" Cotton Yarn Article 75	2 Skeins Red	Steel 00
or		
"STAR" Rug Yarn Article 44	2 Skeins Red	Steel 00
or		
"AUNT LYDIA" Heavy Rug Yarn Article 235	2 Skeins Red	Bone 6
and		
"STAR" Six Strand Embroidery Cotton Article 50	3 Skeins Green 1 Skein Each Brown and Yellow	Steel 4

Directions are given for "STAR" Cotton Yarn and "STAR" Rug Yarn. *"AUNT LYDIA" Heavy Rug Yarn is given in parenthesis.*

TOP SECTION: With Red ch 25 (21), 2 s c in 2nd st from hook, 1 s c in each of the next 4 (3) sts of ch, skip 2 sts of ch, 1 s c in each of the next 4 (3) sts, 2 s c in each of the next 2 sts, 1 s c in each of the next 4 (3) sts, skip 2 sts of ch, 1 s c in each of the next 4 (3) sts, 2 s c in last st, ch 1 to turn each row.

2nd Row. 1 s c in each s c.

3rd Row. Working in s c, increase 1 s c at beginning and 1 s c at end of row.

4th and 5th Rows. Work even.

6th Row. Same as 3rd row.

7th Row. Work even.

8th Row. Increase 1 s c at beginning and end of row, then work 9 (4) rows even.

18th (13th) Row. Decrease 1 s c at beginning and end of row (to decrease: * insert hook in next st, pull loop through, repeat from *, yarn over and pull through all 3 loops at one time).

19th (14th) Row. Work even.

20th (15th) Row. Same as 18th (13th) row. Work 2 rows even.

Next 2 Rows. Decrease 1 s c at beginning and end of each row.

25th (20th) Row. Work even.

26th (21st) Row. Same as 19th (14th) row.

27th (22nd) Row. Decrease in 1st 2 s c, 1 s c in each of the next 6 (4) s c, decrease in next 2 sts, ch 1, turn.

28th (23rd) Row. Decrease 1 s c, 1 s c in each of the next 4 (2) s c, sl st in each of the next 2 sts, break yarn.

Attach yarn in 1st s c on opposite side of 26th (21st) row and working towards the center, repeat 27th (22nd) and 28th (23rd) rows, break yarn.

UNDER SECTION: Work 1st 19 (14) rows same as top section.

20th (15th) Row. Decrease in 1st 2 s c, 1 s c in each of the next 4 s c, ch 7 (6), skip 7 (6) s c for thumb opening, 1 s c in each remaining s c decreasing in last 2 s c.

21st (16th) Row. 1 s c in each s c working 1 s c in each st of ch. Work remaining rows same as front section.

THUMB: With Red work 16 (12) s c around thumb opening and without joining rows, work 6 (3) more rows even.

Next Row. Decrease 4 (3) sts evenly spaced, then work 2 (1) rows even. Decrease every other st until 5 (3) sts remain, break yarn leaving an end. Thread end into needle and draw together; fasten firmly.

With Red crochet the 2 sections together with s c leaving upper edge open for hand but working s c on each section of opening, break yarn.

LEAF: With 12 strands of Green "STAR" Six Strand Embroidery Cotton, ch 21, 1 s c in 2nd st from hook, 1 s c in next st of ch, 1 s d c in each of the next 3 sts of ch (s d c: thread over hook, insert in st, pull through, thread over and pull through all loops at one time), 1 d c in each of the next 3 sts of ch, 1 tr c in each of the next 5 sts of ch, 1 d c in each of the next 3 sts of ch, 1 s d c in each of the next 2 sts of ch, 1 s c in each of the next 2 sts of ch, ch 1 and working on other side of ch, 1 s c in each of the next 2 sts, 1 s d c in each of the next 3 sts, 1 d c in each of the next 2 sts, 1 tr c in each of the next 4 sts, 1 d c in each of the next 2 sts, 1 s d c in each of the next 3 sts, 1 s c in each remaining st.

Next Row. Working around entire leaf, work 1 s c in each s c, 1 s d c in each s d c and 1 tr c in each tr c working 3 s c at point, break thread. Work another leaf in same manner and sew to top of holder as illustrated.

STEM: With Brown using 12 strands, ch 31 and work 30 s c on ch, break thread. Sew to top as illustrated. Using 12 strands of Brown ch 10, s c in 2nd st from hook, 1 s c in next st of ch, 1 s d c in each of the next 5 sts of ch, 1 s c in each of the next 2 sts of ch, break thread and sew to lower edge of top section.

With Yellow using 12 strands, embroider 3 lines on right hand side about 1½ inches long and 2 lines on left hand side about 3½ inches long using an outline st. ✿

Asparagus

MATERIALS:

J. & P. Coats "Knit-Cro-Sheen," Art. A.64, 1 ball each of No. 48 Hunter's Green, No. 26 Nile Green, No. 21 Shaded Greens and No. 126 Spanish Red; or

Clark's O.N.T. Mercerized Bedspread Cotton, Art. B.504, colors of your own choice; or

J. & P. Coats or Clark's O.N.T. Pearl Cotton, Art. A. or B.19, Size 5, 4 balls each of No. 48 Hunter's Green, No. 26 Nile Green and No. 21 Shaded Greens and 1 ball of No. 126 Spanish Red.

Milwards Steel Crochet Hooks No. 4 and No. 7.

A bone ring.

Use thread double throughout.

STALK (Make 6) . . . Starting at tip with Hunter's Green and No. 4 hook, ch 2. **1st rnd:** 8 sc in 2nd ch from hook. Join with sl st to first sc. **2nd rnd:** Ch 3, dc in same place as sl st, 2 dc in each sc around. Join to top of ch-3. **3rd to 7th rnds incl:** Ch 3, dc in each dc around. Join. Break off at end of 7th rnd. **8th to 13th rnds incl:** Attach Shaded Greens to same place as sl st and repeat 3rd rnd. Break off at end of 13th rnd. **14th to 17th rnds incl:** Attach Nile Green to same place as sl st and repeat 3rd rnd. Break off at end of 17th rnd.

Sew stalks together leaving ¾ inch free at rounded end of each stalk.

TIE . . . With a single strand of Spanish Red and No. 7 hook make a chain 2 yards long. **1st row:** Half dc in 3rd ch from hook and in each ch across. Break off.

Wrap tie around asparagus and tie ends into a bow. With Green sc closely around bone ring. Join and break off. Sew bone ring in place. ✿

Shown in color on the inside front cover.

Shown in color on the back cover.

Grapefruit

MATERIALS:

J. & P. COATS "KNIT-CRO-SHEEN," Art. A.64: 1 ball each of No. 1 White and No. 10-A Canary Yellow. . . . A few yards each of No. 126 Spanish Red and No. 12 Black . . . **Milwards Steel Crochet Hook** No. 7. . . . A bone ring.

Starting at center with Canary Yellow, ch 4. **1st rnd:** 11 dc in 4th ch from hook. Join to top of starting chain. **2nd and 3rd rnds:** Ch 3, dc in same place as sl st, 2 dc in each dc around. Join. **4th rnd:** Ch 3, dc in same place as sl st, * dc in next dc, 2 dc in next dc (1 dc increased). Repeat from * around. Join. **5th to 12th rnds incl:** Ch 3, dc in each dc, increasing 12 dc evenly around. Join. Break off at end of 12th rnd.

WHITE SECTION . . . Starting at long side of one strip with White, ch 30, sc in 2nd ch from hook and in each ch across, * ch 44, drop loop from hook, insert hook in first sc made on previous strip and draw dropped loop through, being careful not to twist chain, sc in first 29 ch. Repeat from * until 11 strips in all have been completed, joining last ch 44 to base of first strip as well as first sc on previous strip, then ch 15, drop loop from hook, insert hook at base of first sc made on first strip, draw dropped loop through. Pin White Section in place over Yellow, spacing strips evenly. Still using White and working over ch 15 and end sc of each strip, sc in each dc around, increasing 6 sc evenly around. **Next rnd:** Sc in each sc around, increasing 6 sc evenly around. Join and break off. **Following rnd:** Attach Yellow to same place as sl st, ch 3, dc in each sc, increasing 12 dc evenly around. Join and break off.

CHERRY . . . With Spanish Red, work as for center of pot holder until 2 rnds have been completed. Join and break off. Sew to center. With Black, embroider stem.

Make another piece the same way.

For Padding, see page 2.

Holding 2 pieces together and working through both thicknesses with Yellow, sc closely around. Join and break off. With Yellow, sc closely around bone ring. Sew to pot holder. ✿

Pumpkin

MATERIALS:

J. & P. COATS "KNIT-CRO-SHEEN," **Art. A.64:** 1 ball each of No. 123-A Flamingo and No. 43 Dk. Yellow. . . . A few yards of No. 12 Black . . . **Milwards Steel Crochet Hook** No. 4 . . . A bone ring.

Use 1 strand of Flamingo and 1 strand of Yellow throughout.

Starting at bottom, ch 11. **1st row:** Sc in 2nd ch from hook and each ch across. Ch 1, turn. **2nd row:** 2 sc in first sc (1 sc increased), sc in each sc across, 2 sc in last sc. Ch 1, turn. Repeat 2nd row until there are 44 sc on row. Work without increasing until piece measures 4½ inches. Dec 1 sc at both ends of each row until 10 sc remain—*to dec 1 sc, work off 2 sc as 1 sc.* Break off at end of last row. With a single strand of Flamingo embroider lines on Pumpkin.

EYE (Make 2) . . . Starting at bottom with a single strand of Black and No. 7 hook, ch 12. **1st row:** Sc in 2nd ch from hook and each ch across. Ch 1, turn. **2nd row:** Dec 1 sc at both ends of row. Ch 1, turn. Repeat last row until 3 sc remain. Work off last 3 sc as 1 sc. Break off. Sew Eyes to Head.

NOSE . . . Starting at bottom, ch 10. **1st row:** Sc in 2nd ch from hook and each ch across. Ch 1, turn. Dec 1 sc at beginning of each row until 1 sc remains. Break off. Sew in place.

MOUTH . . . Starting at top with Black, ch 26. **1st row:** Sc in 2nd ch from hook, * 2 sc in next ch, sc in next ch. Repeat from * across. Ch 1, turn. **2nd and 3rd rows:** Dec 1 sc at both ends of row. Ch 1, turn. Break off at end of 3rd row. Sew in place.

Make another piece the same way.

For Padding see page 2.

Sew pieces together. With Black sc closely around bone ring and sew to top.

Shown in color on the inside front cover.

Orange

MATERIALS REQUIRED:
Art. 600 Lily Cotton Yarn Skeins **or**
Art. 930 Sugar 'N Cream Yarn Balls
1 skein or ball Orange **and**
Art. 21 Lily Six Strand Floss
3 skeins Shaded Greens, 2 skeins White and 1 skein Lt. Yellow.
Crochet Hooks Nos. 0 and 5.

ORANGE—With Orange Yarn and No. 0 hook, ch 2, 8 sc in 2d ch from hook. Do not join rows but mark end of each row. **ROW 2**—(2 sc in next sc) 8 times. **ROW 3**—(Sc in next sc, 2 sc in next sc) 8 times. **ROW 4**—(Sc in next 2 sc, 2 sc in next sc) 8 times. (This is an increase in every 3d st). **ROW 5**—Increase in every 4th sc. **ROW 6**—Work even, without increases. Repeat Rows 5 and 6. **ROW 9**—Inc. in every 5th sc. Repeat Rows 6 and 9. **ROW 12**—Inc. in every 6th sc. **ROW 13**—Repeat Row 6. **ROW 14**—Inc. in every 7th sc. **ROW 15**—Inc. in every 12th sc. **ROW 16**—Repeat Row 6. Sl st in next 4 sc. Fasten off.

FLOWER—With White Floss and No. 5 hook ch 5, join with sl st to form ring. **ROW 1**—Ch 1, 10 sc in ring, join to 1st sc. **ROW 2**—* Ch 8, sk 1 ch, sc in next ch,

continued on page 48

Pineapple

MATERIALS:

J. & P. Coats "Knit-Cro-Sheen," Art. A.64, 1 ball each of No. 9 Yellow, No. 17 Shaded Browns and No. 48 Hunter's Green and a few yards of No. 26 Nile Green; or

Clark's O.N.T. Mercerized Bedspread Cotton, Art. B.504, colors of your own choice; or

J. & P. Coats or Clark's O.N.T. Pearl Cotton, Art. A. or B.19, Size 5, 2 balls each of No. 43 Dk. Yellow and No. 48 Hunter's Green; 1 ball each of No. 81 Dk. Brown and No. 26 Nile Green.

Milwards Steel Crochet Hook No. 7.

A piece of felt for lining. A bone ring.

Starting at top of pineapple with Brown, ch 13. Drop Brown. **1st row:** Attach Yellow to first ch from hook, working over Brown, ch 3, 2 dc in same ch (half shell made), skip 2 ch, sc in next ch, skip 2 ch, 5 dc in next ch (shell made), skip 2 ch, sc in next ch, skip 2 ch, 2 dc in next ch, thread over, insert hook in same ch, draw loop through, thread over and draw through 2 loops, drop Yellow, pick up Brown and draw through remaining 2 loops thus changing color (always change color in this manner). Ch 1, turn. **2nd row:** Working over Yellow, sc in first dc, sc in next 2 dc, sc at base of next sc (long sc made), sc in next 2 dc, 3 sc in next dc, sc in next 2 dc, sc at base of next sc, sc in next 2 dc, insert hook in top of starting chain, draw loop through, drop Brown, pick up Yellow, draw through remaining 2 loops on hook. Ch 3, turn. **3rd row:** 2 dc in first sc, sc in next sc, shell in next long sc, sc in center sc of next shell, shell in next long sc, skip 1 sc, sc in next sc, half shell in next sc, drop Yellow, pick up Brown. Ch 1, turn. **4th row:** Sc in first dc, sc in next 2 dc, * long sc over next sc, sc in next 2 dc, 3 sc in next dc, sc in next 2 dc. Repeat from * across, ending with sc in top of turning chain, drop Brown, pick up Yellow. Ch 3, turn. **5th row:** Half shell in first sc, sc in next sc, * shell in next long sc, sc in center sc of next shell. Repeat from * across, ending with shell in last long sc, skip 1 sc, sc in next sc, half shell in last sc, drop Yellow, pick up Brown. Ch 1, turn. **6th to 11th rows incl:** Repeat 4th and 5th rows alternately 3 more times. **12th row:** Repeat 4th row. Ch 1, turn. **13th row:** Sc in first sc, half shell in next long sc, * sc in center sc of next shell, shell in next long sc. Repeat from * across, ending with half shell in last long sc, sc in last sc, drop Yellow, pick up Brown. Ch 1, turn. **14th row:** Long sc in first sc, sc in next 3 dc, * long sc in next sc, sc in next 2 dc. Repeat from * across, ending with long sc in last sc, drop Brown, pick up Yellow. Ch 3, turn. **15th row:** Half shell in first long sc, skip 1 sc, sc in next sc, * long sc in next sc, shell in next long sc. Repeat from * across, ending with half shell in last long sc, drop Yellow, pick up Brown. Ch 1, turn. **16th to 23rd rows incl:** Repeat 12th to 15th rows incl 2 more times. **24th row:** Repeat 4th row, do not ch to turn. **25th row:** Repeat 13th row. **26th to 34th rows incl:** Repeat last 2 rows alternately. Break off at end of 34th row. Make another piece the same way.

LEAF (Make 12) . . . Starting at base with Hunter's Green, ch 13. **1st row:** Sc in 2nd ch from hook and in each ch across. Ch 1, turn. **2nd row:** Skip first sc, sc in each sc across. Ch 1, turn. Repeat 2nd row until 1 sc remains. Break off. Attach Nile Green to side of first row, sc closely across 2 sides, making 3 sc in last sc at point. Break off.

Sew leaves together as shown in illustration. Sew to pot holder. Line pieces of pot holder with felt. Sew pieces together, joining leaves and leaving an opening on one side. With Brown, sc closely around bone ring. Join and break off. Sew in place. ✿

Watermelon

MATERIALS:

J. & P. Coats "Knit-Cro-Sheen," Art. A.64, 1 ball each of No. 46-A Mid Rose, No. 1 White and No. 48 Hunter's Green; or

Clark's O.N.T. Mercerized Bedspread Cotton, Art. B.504, colors of your own choice; or

J. & P. Coats or Clark's O.N.T. Pearl Cotton, Art. A. or B.19, Size 5, 1 ball each of No. 46-A Mid Rose, No. 1 White and No. 48 Hunter's Green; and

J. & P. Coats Six Strand Embroidery Floss, Art. A.11, or **Clark's O.N.T. Six Strand Cotton,** Art. B.11, 1 skein of No. 12 Black.

Milwards Steel Crochet Hook No. 7.

A piece of white felt for lining.

A bone ring.

Starting at center with Mid Rose, ch 4. **1st rnd:** 11 dc in 4th ch from hook. Join. **2nd rnd:** Ch 3, dc in same place as sl st, 2 dc in each dc around. Join to top of ch-3. **3rd rnd:** Ch 3, dc in same place as sl st, * dc in next dc, 2 dc in next dc (1 dc increased). Repeat from * around. Join. **4th to 11th rnds incl:** Ch 3, dc in each dc around, increasing 12 dc evenly on each rnd. Join. Break off at end of 11th rnd. **12th rnd:** Attach White to same place as sl st, ch 3, dc in same place, dc in each dc, increasing 12 dc evenly around. Join. **13th rnd:** Repeat 4th rnd. Join and break off. **14th rnd:** Attach Green to same place as sl st, ch 3, dc in each dc around, increasing 12 dc evenly around. Join. **15th rnd:** Repeat 4th rnd. Join and break off.

With Black Embroidery Floss, embroider lazy daisy sts over rose section to represent seeds. Cut a piece of felt slightly smaller than pot holder. Sew in place on back. Fold pot holder in half and sew ends together for 1 inch. With Green sc closely around bone ring. Join and break off. Sew to pot holder. ✿

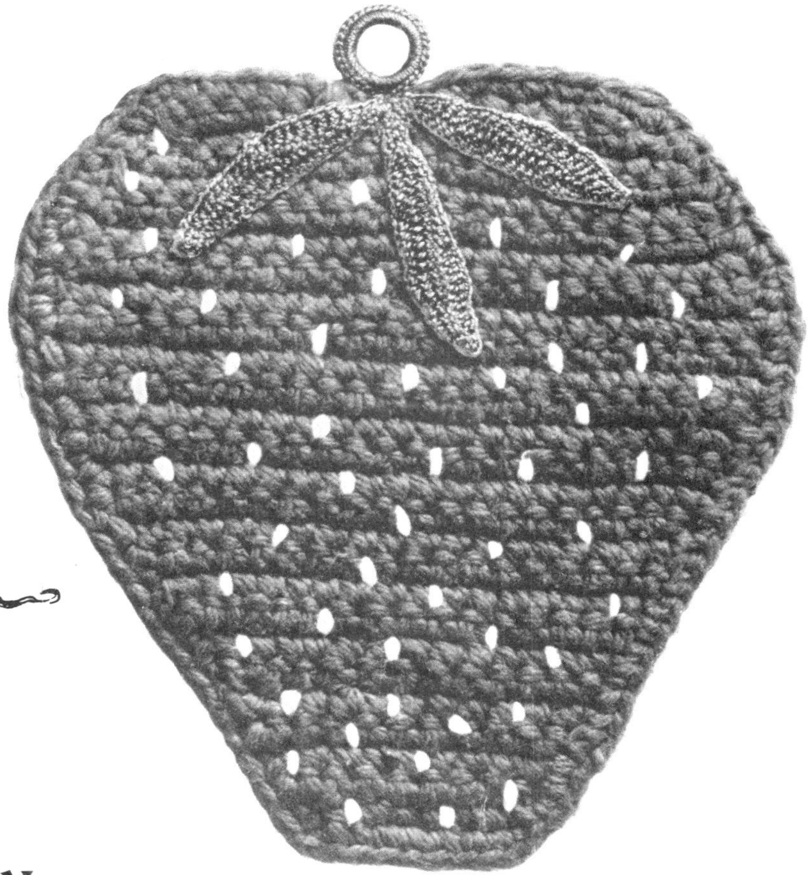

Strawberry

Shown in color on the front cover.

This holder may be made with any of the American Thread Company products listed below:

Material	Quantity	Size of Needle
"STAR" Cotton Yarn Article 75	2 Skeins Red 3 Yards White	Steel 00
or		
"STAR" Rug Yarn Article 44	2 Skeins Red 3 Yards White	Steel 00
or		
"AUNT LYDIA" Heavy Rug Yarn Article 235	2 Skeins Red 3 Yards White	Bone 6
and		
"STAR" Pearl Cotton Article 90, Size 5	1 Ball Green	Steel 7

Directions are given for "STAR" Cotton Yarn and "STAR" Rug Yarn. *"AUNT LYDIA" Heavy Rug Yarn is given in parenthesis.*

FRONT SECTION: With Red ch 7 (5), 2 s c in 2nd st from hook, 1 s c in each of the next 3 (1) sts of ch, 2 s c in each of the next 2 sts of ch, ch 1 to turn all rows.

2nd Row. 2 s c in 1st s c, 1 s c in each remaining s c. Work 1 (1) row even.

4th Row. Working in s c work 3 s c in 1st s c and 2 s c in last s c.

5th Row. 2 s c in 1st s c, 1 s c in each remaining s c.

6th Row. Increase 1 s c at the beginning and end of row.

Next 2 Rows. Same as 5th row.

Next Row. Same as 4th row. Work 3 (1) rows even.

Next Row. Same as 5th row.

Next Row. Same as 4th row.

Next Row. Same as 5th row. Work 3 (3) rows even.

Next Row. Decrease 1 s c at the beginning and end of row (to decrease: insert hook in st, pull loop through, insert hook in next st, pull loop through, yarn over and work off all loops at one time). Work 1 row even.

Repeat the last 2 rows twice (once).

Next Row. Decrease in 1st 2 sts, 1 s c in each of the next 7 (9) s c, sl st in next s c, ch 1, turn.

Next Row. Skip the sl st, decrease in next 2 sts, 1 s c in each of the next 4 (6) s c, decrease in next 2 sts.

Next Row. Decrease in 1st 2 sts, 1 s c in each of the next 3 (5) sts, break yarn.

Next Row. Skip 1 s c from sl st of 24th (20th) row, 1 s c in each of the next 6 (5) s c, decrease in next 2 sts.

Next Row. Decrease in 1st 2 sts, 1 s c in each of the next 3 (2) s c, decrease in next 2 sts.

Next Row. Decrease in 1st 2 sts, 1 s c in next 2 sts, break yarn.

BACK SECTION: Work same as front section.

HULL: With Green ch 26, s c in 2nd st from hook, s c in next st of ch, 1 d c in each of the next 4 sts, 1 tr c in each of the next 12 sts, 1 d c in each of the next 4 sts, 1 s c in each of the next 3 sts, ch 1, turn.

2nd Row. 1 s c in each of the next 4 sts, 1 d c in each of the next 10 sts, 1 s c in each remaining st, break thread.

Work 2 more hull sections in same manner and sew to top of front section as illustrated.

With White embroider seeds on front section using a running st.

With Red crochet the 2 sections together with a row of s c. With Green cover a bone ring with s c and attach to holder as illustrated.

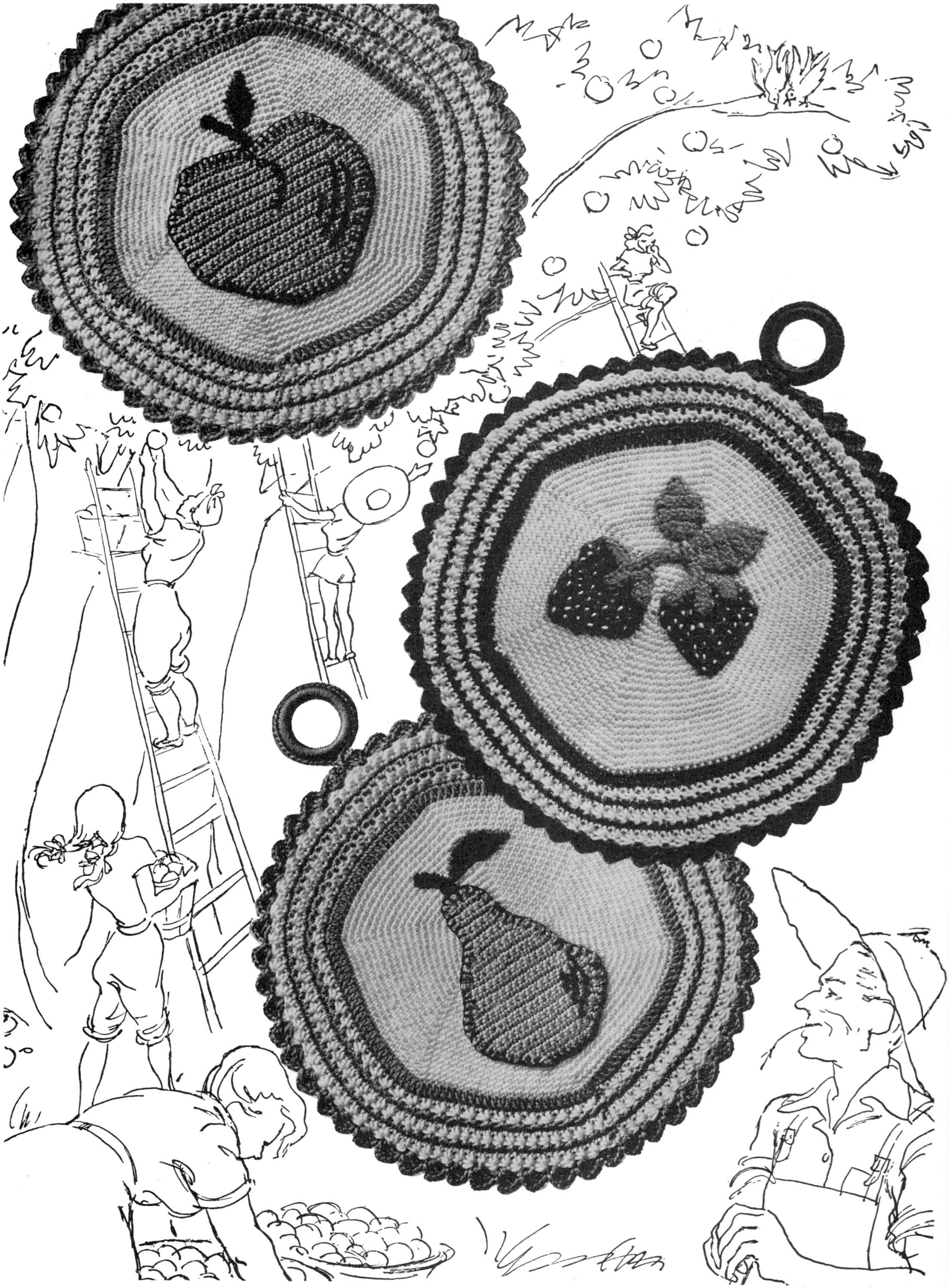

Fruity Pot Holders

Materials Required—
AMERICAN THREAD COMPANY
"DE LUXE" MERCERIZED CROCHET AND KNITTING COTTON, ARTICLE 346
2—250 yd. Balls White.
1—175 yd. Ball each Yellow, Blue and Red,
"STAR" SIX STRAND MERCERIZED EMBROIDERY COTTON, ARTICLE 50
1 Skein each Red, Brown and Green and
"STAR" PEARL COTTON, ARTICLE 90, SIZE 5
1—50 yd. Ball Green.
Steel Crochet Hook No. 8 or No. 9.

Strawberry

With White, ch 2 and work 6 s c in 1st st of ch. (Do not join or turn this or the following rows.)
2nd Row—Place a marker at beginning of rows. Work 2 s c in each s c.
3rd Row—* 1 s c in next s c, 2 s c in next s c, repeat from * all around.
4th Row—* 1 s c in each of the next 2 s c, 2 s c in next s c, repeat from * all around. Continue working in same manner having 1 more st between increasing points in each row, until there are 24 rows (144 s c in 24th row), join with a slip st, drop White.
25th Row—Attach Red (when changing Color always complete last half of st with next Color), ch 3 (counts as 1 d c) and work 1 d c in each of the next 22 s c, 2 d c in next s c, * 1 d c in each of the next 23 s c, 2 d c in next s c, repeat from * 4 times, join in first d c (150 d c), drop Red.
26th Row—Pick up White, ch 3, pick up and pull loop through the 2nd st of ch, pick up the next st of ch and pull loop through, pick up and pull loop through same st as joining, pick up and pull loop through next st leaving all loops on needle, thread over and pull through all loops on needle at one time, ch 1 (the ch 1 is termed the eye of the star st), * pick up and pull loop through the eye of st just made, side loop of st just made and each of the next 2 sts leaving all loops on needle, thread over and pull through all loops at one time, ch 1 (star st), repeat from * all around (75 star sts), join, drop White.
27th Row—Pick up Red, ch 1 and work a row of s c all around working 2 s c in loop of each star st and 1 s c in eye of each star st increasing 1 s c at end of row, join (226 s c).
28th Row—With White, work same as 26th row (113 star sts).
29th Row—With Red, ch 1, 1 s c in loop and 1 s c in eye of each star st, break Red (226 s c).
30th Row—Repeat 28th row, break thread.
Work another section in same manner.
STRAWBERRY: With Red, ch 3, s c in 2nd st from hook, s c in next st of ch, ch 1 to turn each row.
2nd Row—2 s c in each s c.
3rd Row—Working in s c throughout entire berry increase 1 s c in first and last s c.
Repeat 3rd row once, then work 2 rows even.
Next 5 Rows—Repeat 3rd row 3 times, then work 2 rows even.
14th Row—Skip 1 s c, 1 s c in each of the next 11 s c, skip 1 s c, 1 s c in next s c.
15th Row—Skip 2 s c, 1 s c in each of the next 7 s c, skip 2 s c, 1 s c in next s c.
16th Row—Skip 1 s c, 1 s c in each of the next 5 s c, skip 1 s c, s c in next s c, break thread.
Work another berry in same manner.
STEM AND HULL: With Green, ch 8, s c in 2nd st from hook, 1 s c in each remaining st of ch, * ch 5, s c in 2nd st from hook, 1 s c in each remaining st of ch, slip st in base of stem, repeat from * twice, break thread. Work another stem and hull in same manner.
LEAF: Ch 3, s c in 2nd st of ch, s c in next st of ch, ch 1 to turn each row.
2nd Row—2 s c in each s c.
3rd Row—Increase 1 s c in 1st and last s c, then work 3 rows even.
7th Row—Decrease 1 s c at beginning and end of row.
Repeat 7th row once, break thread. Work another leaf in same manner.
With White, embroider seeds in berry as illustrated, sew hull to berry. Sew berries, hulls and leaves to center of holder as illustrated.
EDGE: With Red, crochet the 2 sections together as follows: * ch 3, 3 d c in same space, skip the next star st, s c in loop of next star st, repeat from * all around.
With Red, cover a bone ring with s c and attach to holder as illustrated. ✿

Pear

Front and back sections are worked same as the strawberry pot holder. The border, edge and ring are worked in Blue.
PEAR: With Yellow, ch 9, s c in 2nd st from hook, 1 s c in each remaining st of ch, ch 1 to turn each row.
2nd Row—Increase 1 s c at beginning and end of row.
Repeat 2nd row 5 times, then work 3 rows even.
11th Row—Decrease 1 st at beginning and end of row (To decrease see directions for apple in holder No. 5507).
Repeat 11th row twice, then work 3 rows even.
Repeat 11th row 4 times, then work 5 rows even.
Repeat 11th row twice, break thread.
Use 3 strands of "STAR" Six Strand Mercerized Embroidery Cotton for all embroidery.
With Red, applique pear to front section of holder using a blanket st. Embroider stem in Brown and leaf in Green using a satin st. ✿

Apple

Front and back sections are worked same as the strawberry pot holder. The border, edge and ring are worked in Yellow.
APPLE: With Yellow, ch 9, s c in 2nd st from hook, 1 s c in each remaining st of ch, ch 1 to turn each row.
2nd Row—Working in s c throughout, increase 1 s c at beginning and end of row.
Repeat 2nd row 8 times, then work 8 rows even.
19th Row—Decrease 1 s c at beginning and end of row (To decrease: insert hook in next st, pull through, insert hook in next st, pull through, thread over and pull through all loops at one time).
20th Row—Repeat 19th row, then work 1 row even.
22nd Row—Repeat 19th row.
23rd Row—1 s c in each of the next 9 s c, slip st in each of the next 2 s c, 1 s c in each of the next 9 s c.
24th Row—Repeat last row once, break thread.
Use 3 strands of "STAR" Six Strand Mercerized Embroidery Cotton for embroidery. With Red, applique apple to front section of holder using a blanket stitch. Embroider stem in Brown and leaf in Green using a satin stitch. ✿

Shown in color on the front cover.

Rose Pinwheel

MATERIALS REQUIRED:
Art. 123 Lily Skytone Mercerized Crochet Cotton
1 ball Lt. Green **and**
Art. 39 Lily Pearl Cotton Size 5
1 ball Sunset and ½-ball Salmon Rose
Crochet Hook No. 7.

PINWHEEL—With Green ch 8, join with sl st to form ring. **ROW 1**—Ch 3, 17 dc in ring, join with sl st in ch-3. Work all rows in back lps only. **ROW 2**—Ch 3, dc in same ch-3, 2 dc in each dc around. Join. Repeat once (72 dc). **ROW 4**—Ch 3, dc in next 5 dc, (ch 2, dc in next 6 dc) 11 times. Join. **ROW 5**—Ch 3, dc in same ch-3, (dc in next 5 dc, ch 2, 2 dc in 1st dc in next group) repeated around. Join. **ROW 6**—Ch 3, 2 dc in same ch-3, * dc in next 4 dc, holding back the last lp of each dc on hook, make dc in next 2 dc, yarn over and draw thru all lps on hook (Cluster made), ch 2, 3 dc in 1st dc in next group. Repeat from * around. Join. **ROW 7**—Ch 3, dc in same ch-3, * (2 dc in next dc) twice, dc in each dc across group to 3d from end, dc in 2 end dc made into a decrease, ch 2, 2 dc in 1st dc in next group. Repeat from * around. Join. Repeat twice (thru Row 9). **ROW 10**—Ch 3, dc in same ch-3, * (2 dc in next dc) 3 times, dc in each dc across group to 5th from end, (dc in next 2 dc made into a decrease) twice, ch 2, 2 dc in 1st dc in next group. Repeat from * around. Join. Repeat once. **ROW 12**—Ch 3, dc in same ch-3, * (2 dc in next dc) twice, dc in each dc across group to 5th from end, (dc in next 2 dc made into a decrease) twice, ch 2, 2 dc in 1st dc in next group. Repeat from * around. Join. **ROW 13**—Ch 1, sc in same ch-3, * hdc in next 2 dc, dc in next dc, 2 dc in next dc, (tr in next 2 dc, 2 tr in next dc) twice, tr in next 3 dc, dc in next 3 dc, hdc in next dc, sc in next dc, sc in ch-2, sc in next dc. Repeat from * around. Join. Fasten off.

Edge—Join Sunset to sc between any 2 scallops, ch 1, 4 dc in next sc, (sk 2 sts, 4 dc in next st) 7 times. Now working down left side of same group to center, make (4 dc in side of next row into dc on edge of group) 9 times. Fasten off. Repeat 11 times around circle.

ROSE—With Salmon Rose ch 8, join with sl st to form ring. **ROW 1**—Ch 1, 12 sc in ring. **ROW 2**—Working in back lps only, join to 1st sc, (ch 1, 4 dc in next sc, ch 1, sc in next sc) 6 times. **ROW 3**—(Ch 3, sc behind petals in back lp of sc between next 2 petals) 6 times. **ROW 4**—(Ch 1, 2 dc, 2 tr and 2 dc in next lp, ch 1, sc in sc between petals) 6 times. **ROW 5**—Repeat Row 3 with ch-5 lps. **ROW 6**—(Ch 1, 2 dc, 5 tr and 2 dc in next lp, ch 1, sc in next sc) 6 times. Fasten off. Sew on center circle.

Cover a bone ring with sc in Sunset. Sew between any 2 scallops on edge. Steam and press holder dry on back thru a cloth. Line back with cloth.

Thorn Rose

Materials Required—
AMERICAN THREAD COMPANY
"PURITAN" MERCERIZED CROCHET
AND KNITTING COTTON, ARTICLE 40

1—215 yd. Ball White and

"STAR" PEARL COTTON, ARTICLE 90, SIZE 5

1—50 yd. Ball Red.

2—50 yd. Balls Green will make 2 potholders.

Steel Crochet Hook No. 7.

With White, ch 6, join to form a ring, ch 5, d c in ring, * ch 2, d c in ring, repeat from * 5 times, ch 2, join in 3rd st of ch.

2nd Row—* Ch 4, s c in next d c, repeat from * all around (8 loops), break thread.

3rd Row—Attach Green in loop, * ch 7, s c in 2nd st from hook, 1 s d c in each of the next 2 sts of ch, (s d c: thread over needle, insert in space, pull through, thread over and work off all loops at one time) 1 d c in each of the next 3 sts of ch, s c in next loop, repeat from * all around.

4th Row—1 s c in each of the 5 sts on side of leaf, 3 s c in point of leaf, 5 s c down other side of leaf, repeat from beginning all around, join, break thread.

5th Row—Attach White in point of leaf, 3 s c in same space, * 1 s d c in each of the next 2 s c, d c in next s c, thread over needle twice, insert needle in last s c on side of leaf and work off 2 loops twice, thread over needle once, insert in 1st s c on side of next leaf and work off all loops 2 at a time, skip 2 s c, d c in next s c, 1 s d c in each of the next 2 s c, 3 s c in next s c (top of leaf), repeat from * all around in same manner, join.

6th Row—Ch 3, * 3 d c in next s c, 1 d c in each of the next 3 sts, 1 s d c in each of the next 3 sts, 1 d c in each of the next 3 sts, repeat from * all around in same manner, join in 3rd st of ch, break White.

7th Row—Attach Green at center st at point, ch 1 and work 3 s c in same space, * 1 s c in each of the next 5 sts, ch 9, 1 s c in 2nd st from hook, 1 s d c in each of the next 3 sts of ch, 1 d c in each of the next 4 sts of ch, skip 1 st of previous row, 1 s c in each of the next 5 sts, 3 s c in next st, repeat from * all around in same manner, join.

8th Row—Ch 1 and work 1 s c in same space, 1 s c in each of the next 6 s c, * skip 1 s c and work 7 s c up side of leaf, 3 s c in point of leaf, 7 s c down other side of leaf, skip 1 s c, 1 s c in each of the next 11 s c, repeat from * all around in same manner ending row with 1 s c in each of the last 4 s c, join, break thread.

9th Row—Attach White in center st at point of leaf and work 3 s c in same space, * s c in next s c, 1 s d c in each of the 3 s c, d c in next s c, thread over needle twice, skip 2 s c, insert in next s c, pull through, thread over and work off 2 loops twice, thread over needle once, insert in next s c, pull through and work off all loops 2 at a time, skip 2 s c, d c in next s c, s d c in next s c, s c in next s c, s d c in next s c, d c in next s c, skip 2 s c, thread over needle twice, insert in next st, pull through and work off 2 loops twice, thread over needle once, insert in next s c, pull through and work off all loops 2 at a time, skip 2 s c, d c in next s c on side of next leaf, 1 s d c in each of the next 3 s c, s c in next s c, 3 s c in next s c, repeat from * all around in same manner, join.

10th Row—Ch 3 and work 3 d c in center st at top of each leaf and 1 d c in each remaining st.

11th Row—Ch 3, ** 3 d c in next st (point), 1 d c in each of the next 10 sts, * thread over needle, insert in next st, pull through and work off 2 loops, repeat from *, thread over and work off all loops at one time (a decrease at base of scallop), 1 d c in each of the next 9 d c, repeat from ** all around in same manner.

12th Row—Same as 10th row.

13th Row—Same as last row but decreasing 1 st at base of each scallop, between leaves, break thread.

Work another section in same manner.

With Green, crochet the 2 sections together as follows: ch 3, 2 d c in same space, * skip 1 st, s c in next st, skip 1 st, 3 d c in next st, repeat from * all around, break thread.

With Green, cover a bone ring with s c and attach to pot holder as illustrated. ✿

Roses-in-the-Round

MATERIALS: J. & P. Coats or Clark's O.N.T. Pearl Cotton, *Size 5, 7 balls of White; 3 balls of Red; 2 balls of Green . . . Steel Crochet Hook No. 7.*

Starting at center with White, ch 4. **1st rnd:** 11 dc in 4th ch from hook. Join with sl st in top of starting chain. **2nd rnd:** Ch 1, sc in same place as sl st, sc in each dc around, increasing 7 sc evenly around—*to inc 1 sc, make 2 sc in 1 sc.* **3rd rnd:** Ch 3 and dc in each sc around, increasing 12 dc evenly around—*to inc 1 dc, make 2 dc in 1 sc.* Join. Repeat 2nd and 3rd rnds alternately until piece measures 7 inches in diameter, ending with a dc rnd. Break off. Make another piece same as this.

SMALL ROSETTE (Make 3) . . . With Red, ch 8. Join to form ring. **1st rnd:** Ch 6, (dc in ring, ch 3) 5 times; sl st in 3rd ch of ch-6. **2nd rnd:** In each ch-3 loop make sc, half dc, 3 dc, half dc and sc. Join and break off.

LARGE ROSETTE . . . Work first 2 rnds as for Small Rosette. **3rd rnd:** * Ch 5, sc between 2 sc of next 2 petals. Repeat from * around. **4th rnd:** In each ch-5 loop make sc, half dc, 5 dc, half dc and sc. Join. **5th rnd:** Same as 3rd rnd, making ch-7 (instead of ch-5). **6th rnd:** In each ch-7 loop make sc, half dc, 7 dc, half dc and sc. Join and break off.

SMALL LEAF (Make 12) . . . With Green, ch 8, sc in 2nd ch from hook, half dc in next ch, dc in next 4 ch, 3 dc in next ch; working along opposite side of starting chain, make dc in next 4 ch, half dc in next ch, sc in next ch, sl st in turning chain. Break off.

LARGE LEAF (Make 6) . . . With Green, ch 8, sc in 2nd ch from hook, half dc in next ch, dc in next 2 ch, (2 tr in next ch) twice; 6 tr in next ch; working along opposite side of starting chain, make (2 tr in next ch) twice; dc in next 2 ch, half dc in next ch, sc in next ch. Join and break off.

STEM . . . With Green, make a chain 10 inches long. **1st row:** Sc in 2nd ch from hook, sc in each ch across. Break off.

Place the 2 round crocheted pieces over each other with wrong sides facing and, working over both thicknesses with White, make sc closely around, leaving 6 inches free. Now work sc over remainder of rnd on each piece separately.

EDGING . . . 1st rnd: Attach Red to any sc on outer rnd, sc in same place, * ch 5, skip 3 sc, sc in next sc. Repeat from * around, working over the one thickness only at opening. Join with sl st in first sc. **2nd rnd:** In each sp around make sc, half dc, 3 dc, half dc and sc. Join and break off. Trim one side of Pot holder with Rosettes, Stem and Leaves. Sew a ring at edge. ✿

Roses in-a-Square

MATERIALS: J. & P. Coats or Clark's O.N.T. Pearl Cotton, *Size 5, 7 balls of White; 3 balls of Red; 2 balls of Green . . . Steel Crochet Hook No. 7.*

Starting at center, ch 4. **1st rnd:** 11 dc in 4th ch from hook. **2nd rnd:** Ch 1, 2 sc in same place as sl st, * sc in next 2 dc, 3 sc in next dc. Repeat from * around, ending with sc where the first 2 sc were made. Sl st in first sc. **3rd rnd:** Ch 3, 2 dc in same place as sl st, * dc in each sc to center sc of next 3-sc group, 5 dc in center sc. Repeat from * around, ending with 2 dc where first 2 dc were made. Sl st in top of ch-3. **4th rnd:** Ch 1, 2 sc in same place as sl st, * sc in each dc to center dc of next 5-dc group, 3 sc in center dc. Repeat from * around, ending with sc where first 2 sc were made. Join. Repeat 3rd and 4th rnds alternately until piece measures 6¾ inches square, ending with a dc-rnd. Break off. Make another piece same as this. Place crocheted pieces over each other with wrong sides facing and, working over both thicknesses with White, make sc along 3 sides, then continue making sc on remaining side of each piece separately.

EDGING . . . With Red work 2 rows of Edging same as for Round Pot holder. Make one Large Rosette, 3 Small Rosettes, 6 Large Leaves and 8 Small Leaves as for Round Pot holder. Trim one side as desired. Sew ring at corner. ✿

Beauty Rose

MATERIALS: J. & P. COATS KNIT-CRO-SHEEN, *1 ball each of White and Spanish Red . . . Scraps of Green . . . Steel Crochet Hook No. 7 . . . This amount of material will make three pot holders.*

FRONT . . . Starting at center with Red, ch 6. Join with sl st to form ring. **1st rnd:** Ch 5, (dc in ring, ch 2) 7 times. Join to 3rd st of ch-5 (8 sps). **2nd rnd:** In each sp around make sc, half dc, 3 dc, half dc and sc (8 petals). **3rd rnd:** * Ch 4, sc between next 2 petals. Repeat from * around. **4th rnd:** In each loop around make sc, half dc, 5 dc, half dc and sc. **5th rnd:** Repeat 3rd rnd. **6th rnd:** In each loop around make sc, half dc, 7 dc, half dc and sc. **7th rnd:** Repeat 3rd rnd. **8th rnd:** In each loop around make sc, half dc, dc, 7 tr, dc, half dc and sc. Break off. **9th rnd:** Attach Green to tip of any petal on last rnd of petals, ch 4, holding back on hook the last loop of each tr make 2 tr in same st, thread over and draw through all loops on hook (cluster made), * ch 4, holding back the last loop of each d tr make 3 d tr in same place as last cluster was made, thread over and complete a cluster as before, ch 4, make a 3-tr cluster in same place, ch 7, sc in center tr of next petal, ch 7, make a 3-tr cluster in tip of next petal. Repeat from * around. Join and break off. **10th rnd:** Attach White to any d tr cluster, ch 3, 2 dc in same cluster, * ch 1, 3 dc in next sp, (ch 1, in next sp make 3 dc, ch 1 and 3 dc) twice; ch 1, 3 dc in next sp, ch 1, in next cluster make 3 dc, ch 3 and 3 dc. Repeat from * around, ending with 3 dc in same place as thread was attached, ch 1, dc in 3rd st of starting chain. **11th rnd:** Sl st in sp just formed, ch 3, 2 dc in same sp, * ch 1, 3 dc in next sp. Repeat from * to next corner, ch 1, in corner sp make 3 dc, ch 3 and 3 dc. Work in this manner all around, ending as for previous rnd. Repeat 11th rnd 3 more times. Break off.

BACK . . . With White, ch 5. Join with sl st to form ring. **1st rnd:** Ch 3, 2 dc in ring, (ch 3, 3 dc in ring) 3 times; ch 1, half dc in 3rd st of starting chain. Hereafter pick up only back loop of each dc. **2nd rnd:** Ch 3, dc in sp, * dc in next 3 dc, in corner sp make 2 dc, ch 3 and 2 dc. Repeat from * around, ending with 2 dc in sp. Join as before. **3rd rnd:** Ch 3, dc in sp, * dc in each dc across to corner, in corner make 2 dc, ch 3 and 2 dc. Repeat from * around. Join as before. Repeat 3rd rnd until 10 rnds in all are completed. Break off.

EDGING . . . Place Front and Back pieces together, wrong sides facing. Working through both thicknesses in order to join them, attach Red at corner with Front facing, ch 3, 3 dc in corner, ch 15, sc in 15th ch from hook (loop made), 4 dc in same sp, * (sc in next sp, in next sp make 3 dc, ch 3, sc in 3rd ch from hook—picot made—and 3 dc) 5 times; sc in next sp; in corner make 4 dc, picot and 4 dc. Repeat from * around. Join and break off. ✿

Four Roses

MATERIALS: J. & P. COATS OR CLARK'S O.N.T. PEARL COTTON, *Size 5, 4 balls of White; 1 ball each of Spanish Red, Dark Yellow, Mid Rose and Hunter's Green . . . Steel Crochet Hook No. 7.*

GAUGE: 7 sc make 1 inch; 8 rows make 1 inch.

ROSE (Make 4—1 Rose, 1 Red, 2 Yellow) . . . Starting at center, ch 6. Join with sl st to form ring. **1st rnd:** Ch 6, (dc in ring, ch 3) 7 times; sl st to 3rd ch of ch-6. **2nd rnd:** * In next sp make sc, half dc, 3 dc, half dc and sc (petal made). Repeat from * around. **3rd rnd:** * Ch 5, sc between next 2 petals. Repeat from * around, ending with ch 5. **4th rnd:** In each loop make sc, half dc, 5 dc, half dc and sc. **5th rnd:** * Ch 7, sc between next 2 petals. Repeat from * around. **6th rnd:** In each loop make sc, half dc, 7 dc, half dc and sc. Join and break off.

EDGING—First Rose . . . Attach Green to 4th dc of any petal, ch 5, holding back on hook the last loop of

continued on page 48

Shown in color on the front cover.

Pansy

This holder may be made with any of the American Thread Company products listed below:

Material	Quantity	Size of Needle
"STAR" Cotton Yarn Article 75	1 Skein Each Yellow and Brown 3 Yards Green	Steel 00
or		
"STAR" Rug Yarn Article 44	2 Skeins Yellow 1 Skein Brown 3 Yards Green	Steel 00

With Yellow ch 8, join to form a ring, * ch 3, 3 d c in ring, ch 3, turn.
2nd Row. 2 d c in same space, 3 d c in each of the next 2 d c, 3 d c in end ch, ch 3, turn.
3rd Row. 2 d c in same space, 1 d c in each d c working 3 d c in end ch, ch 3, turn.
4th Row. Same as last row but ch 1 to turn.
5th Row. 1 s c in each of the next 2 sts, 1 s d c in each of the next 2 sts (s d c: yarn over hook, insert in st, pull through, yarn over and pull through all loops at one time), 1 d c in each of the next 12 sts, 1 s d c in each of the next 2 sts, 1 s c in each of the next 2 sts, ch 1, turn. Repeat last row twice, sl st down side of petal, sl st into ring, repeat from * twice, break Yellow.
Attach Brown in ring, ch 3 and work 4 d c in ring, ch 3, turn.

continued on page 47

Sunflower

MATERIALS REQUIRED:
Art. 600 Lily Cotton Yarn Skeins **or**
Art. 930 Sugar 'N Cream Yarn Balls
½-skein or ball each; Orange and Dk. Brown.
Crochet Hook No. 0.

Starting in center with Orange, ch 5, join with sl st to form ring. **ROW 1**—Ch 1, 8 sc in ring, join with sl st in 1st sc, draw out lp, pass ball thru and pull tight. **ROW 2**—Turn, sc in Brown in back lp of 1 sc, * holding back the last lp of each dc on hook, make 2 dc in same sc, yarn over and draw thru all lps on hook (a Cluster-puff st made), sc in back lp of next sc. Repeat from * around (8 puffs), letting Orange hang down on side towards you—out of way. Draw sc down tight between puff sts so the puff sts puff out on back—right side of work. Join with sl st in 1st sc, pull out lp, pass ball thru and pull tight. **ROW 3**—Turn, pull up Orange insert hook in one st, catch Orange and draw thru, ch 1, 2 sc in both lps of each st around (32 sc), letting Brown hang down at back. Join with sl st in 1st sc, draw out lp, pass ball thru and pull tight. **ROW 4**—Turn, draw up Brown and thru both lps of one sc, ch 1, (a 2-dc Cluster-puff st in back lp of next sc, sc in both lps of next sc) repeated around (16 puffs), letting Orange hang down on side towards you. Join Brown

continued on page 48

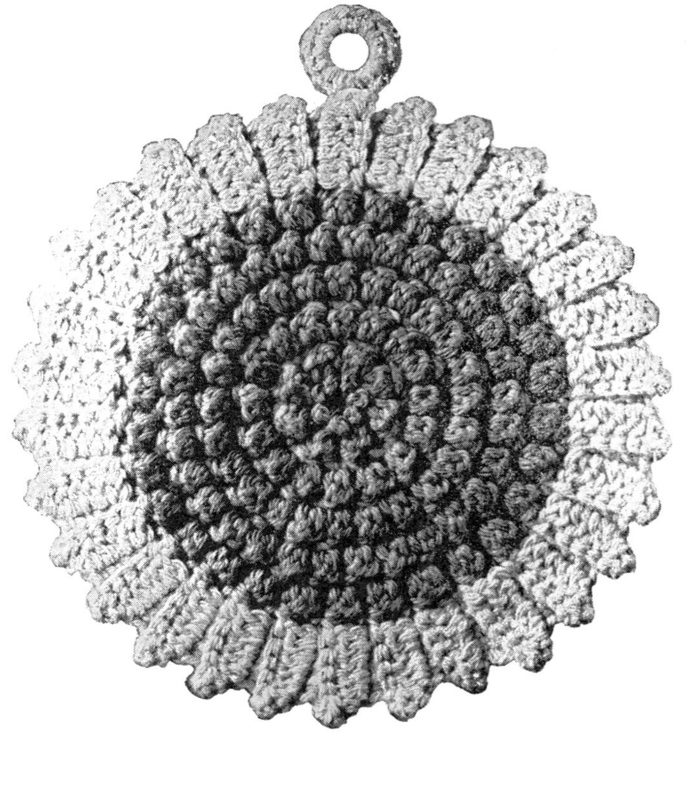

Daisy

MATERIALS:

J. & P. COATS "KNIT-CRO-SHEEN," **Art. A.64:** 1 ball each of No. 1 White and No. 43 Dk. Yellow . . . A few yards of No. 12 Black. Scraps of No. 48 Hunter's Green . . . **Milwards Steel Crochet Hook** No. 7 . . . A bone ring.

FRONT . . . Starting at center with Dk. Yellow, ch 2. **1st rnd:** 7 sc in 2nd ch from hook. **2nd rnd:** 2 sc in each sc around. **3rd rnd:** Sc in each sc, increasing 7 sc evenly around—*to inc 1 sc, make 2 sc in 1 sc.* Repeat 3rd rnd until there are 189 sts on rnd. **Next rnd:** Sc in each sc, increasing 3 sc evenly around (192 sts). Break off.

FIRST PETAL . . . Attach White to any sc. **1st row:** Sc in same place, sc in next 15 sc. Ch 1, turn. **2nd and 3rd rows:** Sc in each sc across. Ch 1, turn. **4th row:** Dec 1 sc—*to dec 1 sc, work off 2 sc as 1 sc*—sc in each sc across. Ch 1, turn. Repeat 4th row until 3 sc remain. **Next row:** Work off 3 sc as 1 sc. Break off.

SECOND PETAL . . . Attach White to next free sc on last Yellow rnd. Sc in same place and complete as for First Petal. Make 10 more Petals in same manner. With Black embroider Face.

BACK . . . Work exactly as for Front, omitting embroidery.

For Padding, see page 2.

With wrong sides facing and working through both thicknesses, attach White to beginning of any Petal, and sc closely around each petal. Join and break off.

With Hunter's Green, make a chain 3 inches long. Sc in each ch across. Break off. Fold chain in half and sew to top of pot holder. With Hunter's Green sc closely around bone ring. Join and break off. Sew to top of loop.

Daffodil

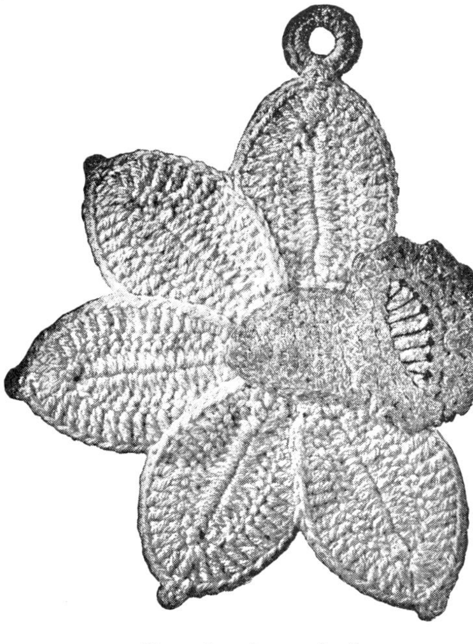

Shown in color on the front cover.

MATERIALS REQUIRED:

Art. 600 Lily Cotton Yarn Skeins **or**
Art. 930 Sugar 'N Cream Yarn Balls
1 skein Yellow and ½-skein Orange **and**
Art. 21 Lily Six Strand Floss
A scrap in Dk. Brown.
Crochet Hook No. 0.

FRONT—Petal—With Yellow ch 13, sk 1 ch, sc in next ch, hdc in next ch, (2 dc in next ch, dc in next ch) 4 times, hdc in next ch, 3 sc in end ch, on other side of ch make hdc in next st, (dc in next st, 2 dc in next st) 4 times, hdc in next st, sc in next st. **ROW 2**—Ch 1, turn, sk sc, sc in next 3 sts, hdc in next 2 sts, dc in next 9 sts, 2 dc in next st, (2 dc, ch 3, sl st in last dc for a p, and 2 dc) in next sc, 2 dc in next sc, dc in next 9 sts, hdc in next 2 sts, sc in next 3 sts, sc in center of end, join to 1st sc. Fasten off. Make 5.

Cup—With Orange ch 2, 3 sc in 2d ch from hook. **ROW 2**—Ch 1, turn, sc in 2 sc, 2 sc in end sc. **ROW 3**—Ch 1, turn, sc in each sc across with 2 sc in end sc. Repeat once. **ROW 5**—Ch 1, turn, sc in each sc. Repeat once. Repeat Row 3 once and Row 5 three times. **ROW 11**—Ch 3, turn, dc in 1st sc, hdc in next sc, sc in next 3 sc, hdc in next sc, 2 dc in next sc, drop Orange, join Yellow thru lp on hook. **ROW 12**—Ch 1, turn and working in back lps only, sc in 1st dc, hdc in next st, dc in next 5 sts, hdc in next st, sc in next st, cut Yellow 2" long, join Orange and working over Yellow end, make sc around base up to other end of last row, 2 sc in 1st Yellow sc, (sc in next st, 2 sc in next st) 4 times, then in front lps of Row 11, make (sc in next st, 2 sc in next st) 5 times. Join to 1st sc. **NEXT ROW**—(Ch 1, dc in next sc, ch 1, sc in next sc) 14 times. Fasten off. With Brown Floss make long sts across Yellow Row 12 with a French Knot at outer end of each st for stamens.

Lap petals and tack tog. Sew Cup in center over base of Petals as illustrated.

BACK—Repeat Front. Sew Front and Back tog. Cover a bone ring with sc in Yellow. Sew to one point. Steam and press dry on back thru a cloth.

Acorn

Materials Required—

AMERICAN THREAD COMPANY
"PURITAN" MERCERIZED CROCHET
AND KNITTING COTTON, ARTICLE 40

1—250 yd. Ball Cream and

"STAR" PEARL COTTON, ARTICLE 90, SIZE 5

4—50 yd. Balls Green will make the Acorn and Leaf Potholders.

Cotton or Kapok for filling.

Steel Crochet Hook No. 8 or No. 9.

With Cream, ch 36, d c in 4th st from hook, 1 d c in each remaining st of ch (ch 3 counts as 1 d c in each row), ch 3 to turn each row.

2nd and 3rd Rows—Working in d c, increase 3 d c at beginning and end of each row.

4th and 5th Rows—Increase 2 d c at beginning and end of each row.

Next 14 Rows—Work even, break thread.

CAP: Attach Green in last d c, ch 5, 1 d c in 4th st from hook, 1 d c in next st of ch, d c in next d c, popcorn st in next st, (popcorn st: 5 d c in same space, drop loop off hook, insert hook in 1st d c and pull loop through, ch 1 to tighten st) * 1 d c in each of the next 2 d c, popcorn st in next st, repeat from * 16 times, d c in next d c, tr c in same space with last d c, work 2 more tr c working each tr c into lower loop of previous st (an increase), ch 1, turn.

2nd Row—Work 1 s c in each st, ch 3, turn (60 s c).

3rd Row—Popcorn st in next st, * 1 d c in each of the next 2 d c, popcorn st in next st, repeat from * 18 times, d c in last st, ch 1, turn.

4th Row—1 s c in each st, ch 1, turn.

5th Row—Sl st over 1st 4 s c, popcorn st in next st, * 1 d c in each of the next 2 sts, popcorn st in next st, repeat from * 16 times, ch 1, turn.

6th Row—1 s c in each st (52 s c), ch 1, turn.

7th Row—Slip st over the 1st 3 s c, popcorn st in next st, * 1 d c in each of the next 2 sts, popcorn st in next st, repeat from * 14 times, ch 1, turn.

8th Row—1 s c in each st (46 s c), ch 1, turn.

9th Row—Slip st over the 1st 3 sts, popcorn st in next st, * 1 d c in each of the next 2 d c, popcorn st in next st, repeat from * 12 times, ch 1, turn.

10th Row—1 s c in each st (40 s c), ch 1, turn.

11th Row—Slip st over the 1st 6 sts, popcorn st in next st, * 1 d c in each of the next 2 sts, popcorn st in next st, repeat from * 8 times, break thread.

With right side of work toward you, attach Cream in 1st d c of 1st row, ch 1 and working across lower edge, work 1 s c in each of the 1st 9 sts, 1 s d c in each of the next 3 sts, (s d c: thread over needle insert in st, pull through, thread over and work off all loops at one time) 1 d c in each of the next 2 sts, 1 tr c in each of the next 2 sts, 1 d tr c (3 times over needle) in each of the next 2 sts, 1 tr c in each of the next 2 sts, 1 d c in each of the next 2 sts, 1 s d c in each of the next 3 sts. 1 s c in each of the next 9 sts, break thread. Work another section in same manner.

Crochet the 2 sections together with a row of s c using Cream on lower sections, pad lightly with cotton or kapok, crochet top sections together in same manner with Green.

With Green, cover a bone ring with s c and attach to top of holder. ✿

Tree

Instructions on next page.

Tree

Materials Required—
AMERICAN THREAD COMPANY
"PURITAN" MERCERIZED CROCHET
AND KNITTING COTTON, ARTICLE 40

1—200 yd. Ball Green and
"STAR" PEARL COTTON, ARTICLE 90, SIZE 5
1—50 yd. Ball White.
Steel Crochet Hook No. 7

With Green, ch 70, d c in 4th st from hook, 1 d c in each remaining st of ch, ch 1, turn (68 d c).

2nd Row—Sl st to next d c, ch 3 and work 1 d c in each d c omitting the last d c, thus decreasing 2 d c in row. Repeat the 2nd row 5 times, ch 5, break thread.

8th Row—Attach White at opposite end and work 1 s c in each of the next 3 d c, * thread over needle, insert needle in top of next st of 6th row and work off as a d c, skip the st in back of the d c, 1 s c in each of the next 4 d c, d c in top of corresponding st of 6th row, skip the st in back of the d c, s c in next st, tr c in top of next st of 5th row, skip the st in back of tr c, s c in next st, d c in top of corresponding st of 6th row, skip the st in back of d c, 1 s c in each of the next 4 d c, repeat from * 4 times, d c in top of st of 6th row, skip the st in back of d c, 1 s c in each remaining d c, break White.

9th Row—Attach Green in 1st s c of last row, ch 7, d c in 4th st from hook, 1 d c in each of the next 3 sts of ch, then work 1 d c in each st across row working 1 d c in each st of ch at end of row, turn.

10th, 11th, 12th, 13th, 14th and 15th Rows—Decrease 1 d c at beginning of each row and 2 d c at end of each row, then ch 4, break thread.

16th Row—Attach White at opposite end and work 1 s c in each of the next 3 d c, * d c in top of st of 2nd row below, skip the st in back of the d c, s c in next d c, tr c in top of st of 3rd row below, skip the st in back of the tr c, s c in next st, d c in top of st of 2nd row below, skip the st in back of d c, 1 s c in each of the next 4 d c, repeat from * across row, break White.

17th Row—Attach Green in 1st s c of last row, ch 6, d c in 4th st from hook, 1 d c in each of the next 2 sts of ch, then work 1 d c in each st across row and 1 d c in each st of ch at end of row.

Repeat the 10th, 11th, 12th, 13th, 14th, 15th, 16th and 17th rows.

Next 5 Rows—Decrease 2 d c at beginning and 2 d c at end of each row, ch 1, turn.

Next Row—Sl st into each of the next 6 d c, ch 3 and work 1 d c in each of the next 12 d c, ch 1, turn.

Next Row—Sl st into each of the next 2 sts, ch 3 and work 1 d c in each of the next 8 d c, ch 1, turn.

Next Row—Sl st into each of the next 2 sts, ch 3 and work 1 d c in each of the next 4 d c, turn.

Next Row—* Thread over needle, insert in next st, pull through, repeat from * twice, thread over and pull through all loops on needle at one time, break thread. Fold in half and mark center st at lower edge for trunk. Attach Green in 4th st from center, ch 3, 1 d c in each of the next 7 sts, ch 3, turn.

Next 2 Rows—1 d c in each d c, break thread.

Work another section in same manner. With White, crochet the 2 sections together with a row of s c working a 4 ch picot at each point. With White, cover a bone ring with s c and attach to holder. ✿

Leaf

SEE *ACORN* FOR MATERIALS.

Starting at A of diagram below with Green, ch 21, dc in 4th st from hook, 1 d c in each remaining st of ch, ch 5, turn.

2nd Row—1 d c in 4th st from hook, 1 d c in next st of ch (an increase of 1 solid mesh at beginning of row), 1 d c in each d c, break thread.

Starting at B, ch 21, d c in 4th st from hook, 1 d c in each remaining st of ch, ch 3 (counts as 1 d c in each row), turn.

3rd Row—1 d c in each d c, 1 tr c in same space with last d c, work 2 more tr c working each tr c into lower loop of previous st (an increase of 1 solid mesh at end of row), ch 14, join to 1st d c of 2nd row of A, break thread.

Attach thread in 1st d c of 2nd row at B end of leaf, ch 3, 1 d c in each of the next 6 d c, ch 2, skip 2 d c, 1 d c in each of the next 13 d c, 1 d c in each of the next 6 sts of ch, ch 2, skip 2 sts of ch, 1 d c in each of the next 6 sts of ch, 1 d c in each remaining d c, ch 3, turn.

4th Row—1 d c in each of the next 6 d c, ch 2, skip 2 d c, 1 d c in each of the next 7 d c, ch 2, skip 2 d c, 1 d c in each of the next 10 d c, ch 2, skip 2 d c, 1 d c in each of the next 7 d c, ch 2, skip 2 d c, 1 d c in each of the next 7 d c, ch 2, skip 2 d c, 1 d c in each of the next 10 sts, ch 3, turn and work back and forth according to diagram, break thread.

With Cream, work another section in same manner working all meshes solid.

With Cream, crochet the 2 sections together with a row of s c.

With Cream cover a bone ring with s c and attach to holder as illustrated. ✿

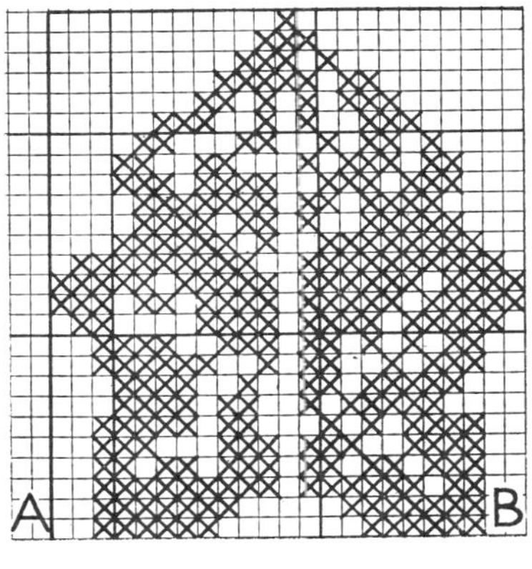

Shown in color on the front cover.

Teapot

MATERIALS: J. & P. COATS CROCHET CORD, *1 ball each of Blue Jewel and Ecru . . . Steel Crochet Hook No. 7 . . . Scraps of red and green felt.*

BODY . . . Starting at bottom with Blue, ch 24 (to measure 3½ inches). **1st row:** 2 sc in 2nd ch from hook, sc in each ch across, 2 sc in last ch. Ch 1, turn. **2nd to 5th rows incl:** 2 sc in 1st sc (an inc), sc in each sc across, 2 sc in last sc (another inc). Ch 1, turn. **6th row:** Sc in each sc across. Ch 1, turn. **7th row:** Same as 2nd row. Repeat 6th and 7th rows alternately until piece measures 3½ inches. Work 5 rows straight. Now dec 1 sc at each end of every other row 3 times—*to dec an sc, work off 2 sc as 1 sc.* Dec 1 sc at each end of every row until 15 sc remain. Break off.

COVER . . . With Blue, ch 2. **1st row:** 6 sc in 2nd ch from hook. Ch 1, turn. **2nd row:** 2 sc in each sc across. Ch 1, turn. **3rd row:** Sc in each sc across. Ch 1, turn. **4th to 14th rows incl:** Sc in each sc across, increasing 2 sts at center of each row about an inch apart. Break off.

RIM . . . With Ecru, ch 6. **1st row:** Sc in 2nd ch from hook and in each ch across. Ch 1, turn. **2nd row:** Sc in each sc across. Ch 1, turn. Repeat the 2nd row until piece measures the length of the last row of Cover. Break off.

KNOB . . . With Ecru, ch 2. **1st rnd:** 6 sc in 2nd ch from hook. **2nd rnd:** 2 sc in each sc around. **3rd rnd:** * Sc in next sc, 2 sc in next sc. Repeat from * around. **4th and 5th rnds:** Sc in each sc around. Break off. Stuff with cotton and sew opening. Double Rim lengthwise and sew along lower edge of Cover. Sew Knob at top of Cover. Sew Cover in place.

HANDLE . . . With double strand of Blue, ch 6. **1st row:** Sc in 2nd ch from hook and in each ch across. Ch 1, turn. **2nd row:** Sc in each sc across. Ch 1, turn. Repeat 2nd row until piece measures 5 inches. Break off. Double piece lengthwise and sew edges together. Sew ends of handle to teapot as shown.

SPOUT . . . With single strand of Blue, ch 10. **1st row:** Sc in 2nd ch from hook and in each ch across. Ch 1, turn. **2nd row:** Sc in each sc across. Ch 1, turn. Repeat the 2nd row until piece measures 2½ inches. Break off. Fold under ¾ inch of this piece (top of spout). Double piece lengthwise and sew edges together for 1 inch. Remainder is base of Spout. Sew base of Spout in place and tack free part in shape. Cut 3 cherries of red felt and 3 double leaves of green. Appliqué in place. For padding, see page 2. ✿

Morning, Noon and Night

Any of these holder sets can be made from a ball of White Enterprise Yarn and approximately 50 yards of color matching the kitchen decorations.

These clocks, each with hands set at different hours, make a holder for each meal of the day.

Crochet firmly to get a heavy holder. Diameter 5¾ to 6 in. The directions are for White faces—for the colored face reverse colors.

ROUND 1: With White ch 5, sl st to form a ring, ch 1.

ROUND 2: 9 sc in ring. Work around center.

ROUND 3: 2 sc in each st around (20 sc).

ROUND 4: Sc in next 2 sc, 2 sc in next.

Repeat around. Continue with sc, inc when necessary, to keep flat (do not over inc or will pucker) until 13 rounds are made. Fasten off.

EDGE: Join color to White face in back loop of st, sl st in back loop of each st around. Fasten off. Numerals and hands are crocheted and sewed in place (as illustrated). Colored numbers are made for White faces or White for colored faces. All may be embroidered if desired.

The hands and numerals are simple chains, crocheted to the proper length—for No. 1, ch 5—No. 2, ch 12—No. 3, ch 16—No. 4, ch 15—No. 5, ch 12—No. 6, ch 12—No. 7, ch 9—No. 8, ch 16—No. 9, ch 13—No. 0, ch 8. For hands, 6 and 8 o'clock, ch 20. Noon, ch 14. Pointer on end of hands, ch 6. Applique in place as shown with hands pointing to hours desired. Ch 6 and join to form ring to sew to center of clock over inner end of hands. Crochet a loop or sew a bone ring above 12 on each. ✿

Broom

MATERIALS: J. & P. COATS OR CLARK'S O.N.T. PEARL COTTON, *Size 5, 3 balls of Ecru and 1 ball of Steel Blue. Scraps of Red and Black . . . Steel Crochet Hook No. 7 . . . A bone ring.*

Starting at side of broom with Ecru, ch 40 to measure about 4½ inches. **1st row:** Sc in 2nd ch from hook and in each ch across. Ch 1, turn. **2nd row:** Picking up back loop only, make sc in each sc across. Ch 1, turn. Repeat 2nd row until 53 rows are completed.

TOP . . . 1st row: Working along side, make sc in first st of every other row across (27 sc across row). Ch 1, turn. **2nd row:** Make sc in each sc across. Ch 1, turn. **3rd row:** Dec 1 sc, sc in each sc across, dec 1 sc at end of row—*to dec 1 sc, work off 2 sc as 1 sc.* Ch 1, turn. Repeat 3rd row until 11 rows are completed (9 sc on 11th row). Break off.

HANDLE . . . 1st row: Attach Blue to first sc and make sc in each sc across. Ch 1, turn. **2nd row:** Sc in each sc across. Ch 1, turn. Repeat 2nd row until handle measures 5 inches. Break off.

Embroider 7 rows along top of ribbing, using Blue and Red alternately. Embroider short Black scattered lines between ribs. Make another piece same as this. Sew pieces together, padding bottom. Sew bone ring to handle. ✿

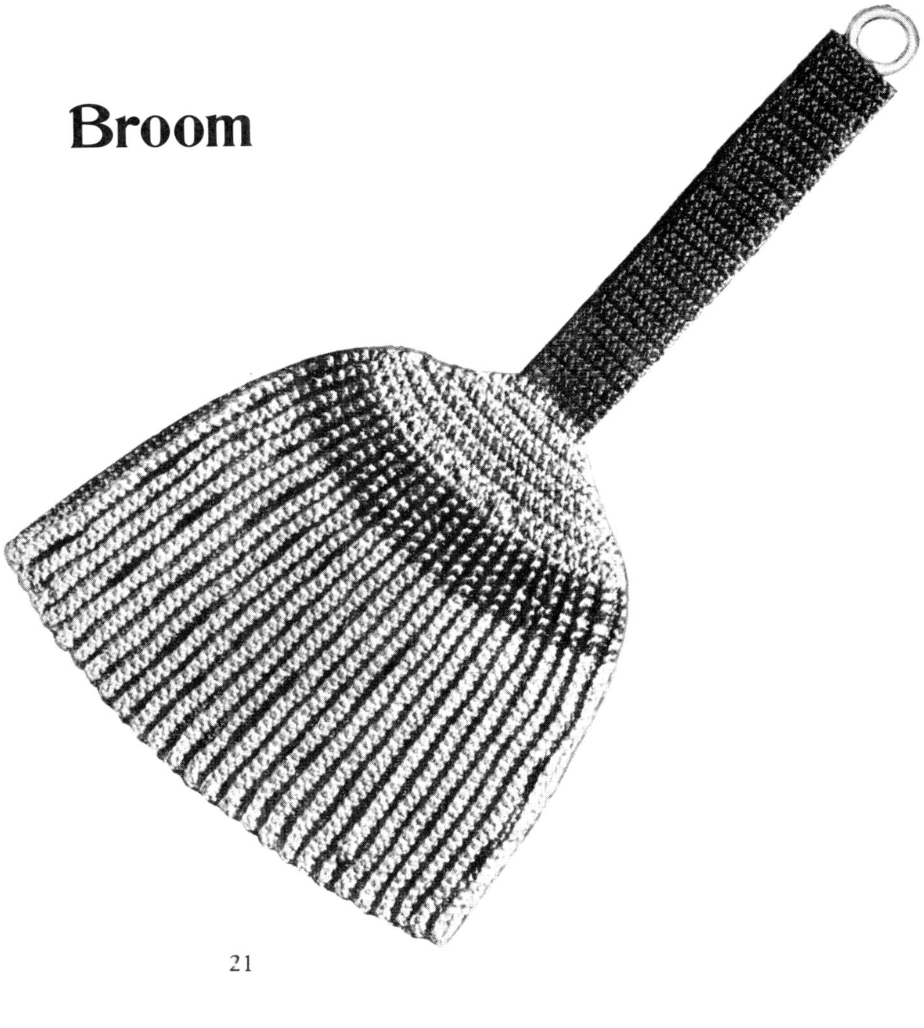

Cookie Jar

Tea Time!

Materials Required—
AMERICAN THREAD COMPANY
"PURITAN" MERCERIZED CROCHET AND
KNITTING COTTON, ARTICLE 40

3—160 yd. Balls Yellow and
"STAR" PEARL COTTON, ARTICLE 90, SIZE 5
4—50 yd. Balls Blue will make Jar, Plate and Teapot Holders.
Steel Crochet Hook No. 7.

With Yellow, ch 21, s c in 2nd st from hook, 1 s c in next st of ch, * ch 1, skip 1 st of ch, 1 s c in each of the next 2 sts of ch, repeat from * across row, ch 2, turn.
2nd and 3rd Rows—2 s c in 1st s c (an increase), ch 1, 2 s c in next s c, * ch 1, skip 1 s c, 2 s c in next s c, repeat from * across row, ch 2, turn.
4th and 5th Rows—Skip 1st s c, 2 s c in next s c, * ch 1, skip 1 s c, 2 s c in next s c, (pattern) repeat from * across row, ch 2, turn.
6th Row—Increase 1 pattern at beginning of row, then work even in pattern to within the last pattern, ch 1, 2 s c in 1st s c of last pattern (an increase), 2 s c in next s c of last pattern, ch 2 to turn each row.
Work 3 rows even in pattern.
10th Row—Increase 1 pattern at beginning and end of row, then work 5 rows even in pattern.

continued on next page

16th Row—Same as 10th row, then work 3 rows even in pattern.
20th Row—Same as 10th row, then work 5 rows even in pattern.
26th Row—Same as 10th row, then work 4 rows even in pattern, break Yellow.
31st Row—Attach Blue and work 10 rows even in pattern, break Blue.
41st and 42nd Rows—With Yellow, decrease 1 pattern at end of each row.
Next 4 Rows—Work even in pattern.
47th and 48th Rows—Same as 41st and 42nd rows, then work 2 rows even.
51st Row—Decrease 1 pattern at beginning and end of row.
52nd Row—Work even in pattern across row, then ch 5 for lid, turn.
53rd Row—2 s c in 3rd st from hook, ch 1, skip 1 st of ch, 2 s c in next st of ch, ch 1, then work in pattern across row, ch 5, turn.
54th Row—Work on ch same as opposite side, then work even in pattern across row, ch 2, turn.
55th Row—Work even, ch 2, turn.
56th Row—Skip 1st s c, sl st in each of the next 2 s c, ch 1, 2 s c in next s c, then work in pattern across row to within the last pattern, ch 1, sl st in 1st s c of last pattern, ch 2, turn. Repeat the last row 5 times, break thread. Work another section in same manner.
On top section, with Blue, outline the lid as illustrated and embroider knob on lid using a satin stitch.
With Yellow, working on Blue band, embroider flowers using a lazy daisy stitch with French knot in center.
With Blue, crochet the 2 sections together as follows: attach thread, * ch 3, 2 d c in same space, skip the length of a d c, sl st in next st, repeat from * all around.
HANDLES: With Blue, ch 32 and work 30 s d c on ch (s d c: thread over needle, insert in st, pull through, thread over and pull through all loops at one time), break Blue. Attach Yellow at lower edge and work 1 s c in each st. Attach to holder as illustrated.
With Yellow, cover a bone ring with s c and attach to back of holder. ✿

Floral Teapot

Work first 51 rows same as jar potholder.
52nd and 53rd Rows—Decrease 1 pattern at beginning and end of each row (10 patterns left).
Next 5 Rows—Work even in pattern, ch 1, turn.
Next Row—1 s c in each s c (20 s c) ch 1, turn.
Next Row—1 s c in each s c, ch 1, turn.
Next 4 Rows—Decrease 1 s c at beginning and end of each row.
Next Row—Decrease 1st s c, s c in next s c, 1 s d c in each of the next 2 sts, 1 d c in each of the next 4 sts, 1 s d c in each of the next 2 sts, s c in next st, break thread.
Work another section in same manner.
SPOUT: With Yellow, ch 2, 2 s c in 2nd st from hook, ch 1, turn.
2nd Row—1 s c in each s c, ch 1, turn.
3rd Row—Working in s c, increase 1 s c at end of row, ch 1, turn.
4th Row—Increase 1 s c at beginning of row, ch 1, turn.
5th Row—Same as 3rd row, ch 2, turn.
6th Row—S d c in same space, 1 d c in next st, 1 s c in each of the next 3 sts, ch 1, turn.
7th Row—1 s c in each of the next 3 sts, s d c in next st, 2 s d c in last st, ch 2, turn.
8th Row—1 s d c in each of the next 2 sts, 1 s c in each of the next 4 sts, ch 1, turn.
9th Row—1 s c in each of the next 3 sts, 1 s d c in each of the next 2 sts, 2 d c in end st, ch 1, turn.
10th Row—1 s c in each st, break Yellow.
11th Row—With Blue, ch 1, 1 s c in each of the next 2 sts, ch 1, skip 1 st, 1 s c in each of the next 2 sts, ch 1, skip 1 st, 2 s c in end st, ch 2, turn. Work 9 rows even in pattern same as on large section, break Blue.
21st Row—Attach Yellow, 1 s c in each of the next 2 s c, 1 s c in next ch 1, 1 s c in each of the next 2 s c, 1 s c in next ch 1, 1 s c in next s c, 2 s c in last s c, ch 2, turn.
22nd Row—S d c in same space, 1 s c in each remaining st decreasing 1 s c at end of row, ch 1 turn.
23rd Row—Decrease 1 s c at beginning of row, 1 s c in each s c, increasing 1 s c at end of row, ch 1, turn. Work 2 rows even in s c.
26th, 27th and 28th Rows—Working in s c decrease 1 s c at beginning and end of each row, ch 1, turn.
29th Row—* Insert needle in next st, pull through, repeat from * once, thread over and pull through all loops on needle at one time, break thread. Work another spout in same manner.
HANDLE: Ch 38 and work same as jar handle.
With Yellow and working on top section embroider flowers in the Blue band same as on jar.
Sew spout to each section.
With Blue, outline lid as illustrated. With Blue, crochet the 2 sections together same as jar holder.
With Blue, cover a bone ring with s c and attach to holder. ✿

Plate

With Yellow, ch 6, join to form a ring, ch 1 and work 8 s c in ring, do not join this or the following rows. Place a marker at beginning of each row.
2nd Row—2 s c in each s c.
3rd Row—* 1 s c in next s c, 2 s c in next s c, repeat from * all around.
4th Row—Working in s c, increase in every 3rd s c.
5th Row—Increase in every 4th s c.
6th Row—Increase in every 5th s c, then work 1 row even.
8th Row—Increase in every 6th s c.
9th Row—Increase in every 7th s c, then work 1 row even.
11th Row—Increase in every 8th s c.
12th Row—Increase in every 9th s c, then work 1 row even.
14th Row—Increase in every 10th s c.
15th Row—Increase in every 11th s c.
16th Row—Increase in every 12th s c.
17th Row—Increase in every 8th s c, then work 3 rows even.
21st Row—Increase in every 9th s c, sl st in each of the next 2 s c to even row, break Yellow.
22nd Row—Attach Blue, ch 1, 1 s c in same space, 1 s c in next s c, * ch 1, 1 s c in each of the next 2 s c, repeat from * all around, sl st in ch 1 to join.
23rd Row—Ch 1, skip 1st s c, 2 s c in next s c, * ch 1, skip the ch 1 and 1 s c, 2 s c in next s c, repeat from * all around, ch 1, sl st in 1st ch 1 to join. Repeat the last row 6 times, break Blue.
30th Row—Attach Yellow and work 1 s c in each s c and 1 s c in each ch 1, join, break thread. Work another section in same manner. On top section, with Yellow embroider flowers as illustrated, using a lazy daisy stitch with French knots in the center and working in the Blue stripe only. With Blue, embroider a large flower in center using a lazy daisy st with Yellow French knot in center.
With Blue, crochet the 2 sections together as follows: * ch 3, 2 d c in same space, skip 2 s c, sl st in next s c, repeat from * all around. With Blue, cover a bone ring in s c and attach to holder. ✿

Hobby Horse

This holder may be made with any of the American Thread Company products listed below:

Material	Quantity	Size of Needle
"STAR" Cotton Yarn Article 75	2 Skeins Beige	Steel 00
or		
"STAR" Rug Yarn Article 44	2 Skeins Beige	Steel 00
or		
"AUNT LYDIA" Heavy Rug Yarn Article 235	1 Skein Beige	Bone 6
and		
"STAR" Six Strand Embroidery Cotton Article 50	4 Skeins Brown 1 Skein Each Red, Yellow and Green	Steel 4

Directions are given for "AUNT LYDIA" Heavy Rug Yarn. *"STAR" Rug Yarn and "STAR" Cotton Yarn are given in parenthesis.*

With Beige ch 6 (11), 2 s c in 2nd st from hook, 1 s c in each of the next 3 (8) sts of ch, 2 s c in next st of ch, ch 1 to turn all rows.

2nd Row. Working in front loop of st, 2 s c in 1st s c, 1 s c in each remaining s c.

3rd Row. Working in back loop of st, 2 s c in 1st s c, 1 s c in each remaining s c.

The remainder of potholder is worked in same manner alternating 1 row worked in front loop, 1 row worked in back loop and will not be referred to again. The ribbed side will be the inside of work.

4th Row. 2 s c in 1st s c, 1 s c in each of the next 6 (11) s c, decrease 1 s c in next 2 sts (to decrease: insert hook in st, pull loop through, insert hook in next st, pull loop through, yarn over and work off all loops at one time).

5th Row. Working in s c, increase 1 s c at end of row.

6th Row. Increase 1 s c at beginning of row, 1 s c in each remaining s c. Work 1 (1) row even.

Repeat the last 2 (2) rows twice (3).

12th (14th) Row. Increase 1 s c at the beginning of row and decrease 1 s c at end of row. Work 1 (3) row even.

14th (18th) Row. 1 s c in each of the 1st 12 (17) s c, sl st in next st, ch 4 (6), turn.

15th (19th) Row. 3 s c in 2nd st from hook, 1 s c in each of the next 2 (4) sts of ch, 1 s c in next sl st, 1 s c in each remaining s c.

16th (20th) Row. 1 s c in each of the 1st 17 (25) s c.

17th (21st) Row. Decrease 1 s c at end of row.

18th (22nd) Row. Decrease 1 s c at beginning of row, 1 s c in each remaining s c. Work 1 (3) row even.

20th (26th) Row. Same as 18th (22nd) row.

21st (27th) Row. Same as 17th (21st) row.

22nd (28th) Row. Same as 18th (22nd) row.

23rd (29th) Row. 1 s c in each of the 1st 9 (16) sts, decrease in next 2 sts.

24th (30th) Row. Same as 18th (22nd) row.

25th (31st) Row. 1 s c in each of the 1st 6 (12) sts, decrease in next 2 sts.

26th (32nd) Row. Skip 1 st, decrease in next 2 sts, 1 s c in each remaining s c, break yarn.

EAR: Ch 8 (12), sl st in 2nd st from hook, 1 s c in each remaining st of ch, ch 1 to turn all rows.

2nd Row. Working in back loop, 2 s c in 1st s c, 1 s c in each of the next 3 (7) s c, decrease in next 2 sts.

3rd Row. Working in front loop, decrease in 1st 2 sts, 1 s c in each of the next 3 (6) sts, 2 s c in next st.

4th Row. 2 s c in 1st s c, 1 s c in each of the next 2 (7) sts, sl st in next st.

5th Row. Skip 1 st, decrease in next 2 sts, 1 s c in each remaining s c, break yarn.

Starting at the 13th row of head, sew ear to top of head as illustrated. Work another section in same manner.

Starting at right hand side of straight edge of neck overcast the 2 sections together working 1 inch beyond ear and leaving about 13 rows free on opposite side for opening.

MANE: Cut 18—5 inch lengths. Take 1 length, loop through st, draw ends through tightly.

Start at 2 sts before ear, work in back of ear and down side of head. Trim as illustrated.

Overcast mane to back of ear to hold in position.

BRIDLE IS MADE TO FIT: With Brown "STAR" Six Strand Embroidery Cotton ch 7, s c in 2nd st from hook, 1 s c in each remaining st of ch, ch 1 to turn all rows.

2nd Row. Work 1 s c in each s c. Repeat 2nd row a sufficient number of times for strip to go across mouth. Sew in position. Crochet another strip in same manner to fit from top of head to 1st strip, ending with 1 s c in each of the 1st 4 s c, sl st in next s c.

Next Row. Skip the sl st, 1 s c in each remaining s c.

Next Row. 1 s c in each of the 1st 2 s c, sl st in next s c.

Next Row. Skip the sl st, 1 s c in each remaining s c, break thread. Sew the slanted edge to 1st strip. Crochet a 3rd strip in same manner as 2nd strip to fit from 2nd strip to lower part of head sewing slanted edge to 2nd strip. Crochet a 4th strip in same manner as 1st strip to fit from 2nd strip to top of head. Sew in position.

REIN: With Brown ch 3, s c in 2nd st from hook, ch 1, turn.

2nd Row. S c in s c, ch 1, turn. Repeat 2nd row until rein measures about 9 inches or desired length, break thread. Sew in position as illustrated.

DECORATION FOR BRIDLE: With Red ch 6, s c in 2nd st from hook, 1 s c in each remaining st of ch, ch 1, turn.

2nd Row. 1 s c in each s c, ch 1, turn. Repeat 2nd row 4 times, break thread. Work another square in same manner. Sew in position.

With Green work 2 more squares in same manner but ch 4 in beginning and work only 3 rows.

Sew 1 Green square on top of each Red square.

With Yellow ch 3, s c in 2nd st from hook, 5 s c in same space, join, break thread leaving an end long enough to sew in position. Work 11 more rings in same manner.

With Brown, cover a bone ring with s c and sew in back of ear. ✿

Perky Pig

This holder may be made with any of the American Thread Company products listed below:

Material	Quantity	Size of Needle
"DE LUXE" Crochet Cotton Article 346	2 Balls White	Steel 3
or		
"PURITAN" Crochet Cotton Article 40	2 Balls White	Steel 3
and		
"STAR" Six Strand Embroidery Cotton Article 50	2 Skeins Pink and 1 Skein each Blue, Red, Yellow, Green and Black	Steel 8

Entire potholder is made with a double strand of cotton. With White and No. 3 hook, ch 12, s c in 2nd st from hook, 1 s c in each remaining st of ch, ch 1, turn.
2nd Row. 2 s c in each of the next 2 s c, 1 s c in each of the next 7 s c, 2 s c in each of the next 2 s c, ch 1, turn.
3rd Row. 2 s c in each of the next 2 s c, 1 s c in each of the next 11 s c, 2 s c in each of the next 2 s c, ch 1, turn.
4th and 5th Rows. Working in s c throughout, increase 1 s c at beginning and end of row, ch 1, turn.
Next 3 Rows. Work even.
9th and 10th Rows. Repeat 4th row.
Next 2 Rows. Work even.
13th Row. 1 s c in each of the next 27 s c, ch 5, turn.
14th Row. S c in 2nd st from hook, 1 s c in each of the next 3 sts of ch, 1 s c in each remaining s c, ch 1, turn.
15th Row. Increase 1 s c at beginning of row, ch 1, turn.
Next 4 Rows. Work even.
20th Row. Repeat 4th row.
21st Row. 2 s c in next s c, 1 s c in each of the next 29 s c, ch 1, turn.
Next 8 Rows. Work even.
30th Row. Ch 5, turn, s c in 2nd st from hook, 1 s c in each remaining st of ch, 1 s c in each s c, ch 1 to turn each of the following rows.
Next 4 Rows. Work even.
35th and 36th Rows. Decrease 1 s c at end of row (to decrease: insert hook in st, pull through, insert hook in next st, pull through, thread over and pull through all loops at one time).
37th Row. 1 s c in each of the next 28 s c.
38th Row. Repeat 35th row.
39th Row. Increase 1 s c at end of row.
40th Row. Increase 1 s c at beginning of row.
41st Row. 1 s c in each of the next 27 s c.
42nd Row. Repeat 35th row.
43rd Row. Decrease 1 s c at beginning of row.
44th and 45th Rows. Decrease 1 s c at beginning and end of each row.
46th Row. Work even.
47th Row. Repeat 39th row.
48th Row. Work even.
49th Row. Decrease 1 s c, 1 s c in each of the next 17 s c.
50th and 51st Rows. Repeat 44th row.
52nd Row. 1 s c in each of the next 8 s c.
53rd Row. Sl st in each of the next 3 s c, 1 s c in each of the next 5 s c, without breaking thread work a row of s c all around entire section.
TAIL: With White ch 13, s c in 2nd st from hook, 1 s c in each remaining st of ch, break thread. Sew tail in position.
EARS: With Pink "STAR" Six Strand Embroidery Cotton and No. 8 hook, ch 11, s c in 2nd st from hook, 1 s c in each remaining st of ch, ch 1 to turn each row.
Work 3 rows even, then decrease 1 s c at beginning and end of each row until 1 st remains, break thread.
Work 3 more sections in same manner. Sew 2 sections together and sew in position as illustrated.
SNOUT: With Pink ch 5, s c in 2nd st from hook, 1 s c in each remaining st of ch.
2nd Row. Increase 1 s c at beginning and end of row.
Work 3 rows even. Decrease 1 s c at beginning and end of each row until 1 st remains, break thread leaving an end for sewing. Thread into needle and sew in position.
FLOWERS: With Yellow "STAR" Six Strand Embroidery Cotton and No. 8 hook, ch 2, 10 s c in 2nd st from hook, join, break thread. Attach Blue, * ch 3, 3 d c in same space, ch 3, sl st in same space, skip 1 s c, sl st in next s c, repeat from * 4 times, break thread.
Work 1 more flower in Blue and 2 flowers in Red.
LEAVES: With Green "STAR" Six Strand Embroidery Cotton ch 10, d c in 3rd st from hook, 1 d c in each of the next 4 sts of ch, 1 s c in each of the next 2 sts, 3 s c in next st, working on other side of ch, 1 s c in each of the next 2 sts, 1 d c in each of the next 5 sts, break thread. Work 4 more leaves in same manner. Sew flowers and leaves in position as illustrated. With Green and using 12 strands for all embroidery, embroider stem in chain st. With Black, embroider eye, ears, mouth and snout.
BACK SECTION: Work 1st 33 rows same as front.
34th Row. 1 s c in each of the next 5 s c, ch 10, skip 10 s c (thumb opening), 1 s c in each remaining s c.
35th Row. 1 s c in each s c and 1 s c in each st of ch, decreasing 1 s c at end of row. Complete back section same as front.
THUMB: With White and No. 3 hook, work 1 s c in each st of thumb opening (20 s c), without joining rows work 11 rows in s c even.
Next Row. Decrease 5 s c evenly spaced, then work 3 rows even.
Decrease every other st until 8 sts remain, break thread leaving an end. Thread into needle and sew top of thumb together, fasten firmly.
Overcast sections together leaving an opening around head large enough for hand.
Cover a bone ring with s c and attach to back of holder 1 inch from top of back. ✿

Birdcage

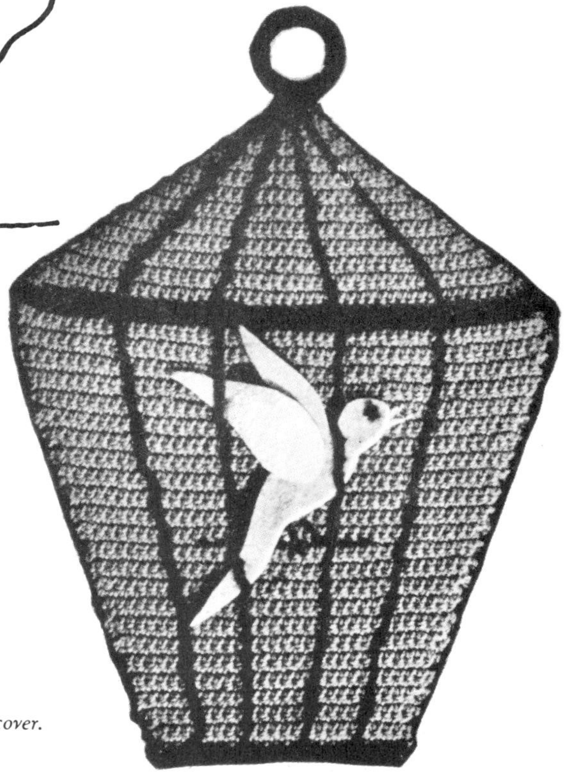

Shown in color on the inside front cover.

MATERIALS:

J. & P. COATS "KNIT-CRO-SHEEN," Art. A.64: 1 ball of No. 70 Blue Jewel . . . A few yards of No. 12 Black . . . **Milwards Steel Crochet Hook** No. 7 . . . A piece of yellow felt . . . A bone ring.

Starting at top of Cage with Blue Jewel, ch 2. **1st row:** 5 sc in 2nd ch from hook. Ch 1, turn. **2nd row:** 2 sc in first sc, sc in next 3 sc, 2 sc in next sc. Ch 1, turn. **3rd to 24th rows incl:** 2 sc in first sc, sc in each sc across, 2 sc in last sc. Ch 1, turn. **25th and 26th rows:** Sc in each sc across. Ch 1, turn. **27th row:** Dec 1 sc *—to dec 1 sc, work off 2 sc as 1 sc—* sc in each sc across to within last 2 sc, dec 1 sc. Ch 1, turn. Repeat last 3 rows until 25 sc remain on last row. Break off. Attach Black and sc in each sc across. Ch 1, turn. Sc in each sc across. Break off.

Cut out felt bird, pin in place.

BAR (Make 4) . . . Cut 3 strands of Black about 10 inches long. Sew in place over Bird to shape top and bottom of Cage. Embroider bird's eye, feet and stick with Black, embroider bill with a scrap of Flamingo. With Black make a chain to reach across widest part of Cage, sc in 2nd ch from hook and in each ch across. Break off. Sew in place. Cut 3 strands of Black to reach around outer edge of Cage. Sew in place as before.

Make another piece the same way.

For Padding, see page **2.**

With Black sc closely around bone ring. Join and break off. Sew to top of Cage. ✿

Chicken

MATERIALS:

J. & P. Coats "Knit-Cro-Sheen," Art. A.64, 1 ball each of No. 78 Turquoise and No. 32 Purple and a few yards of No. 126 Spanish Red and No. 12 Black; or

Clark's O.N.T. Mercerized Bedspread Cotton, Art. B.504, colors of your own choice; or

J. & P. Coats or Clark's O.N.T. Pearl Cotton, Art. A. or B.19, Size 5, 4 balls of No. 24-D Aqua, 2 balls of No. 18-D Shaded Dk. Purples and a few yards of No. 126 Spanish Red and No. 12 Black.

Milwards Steel Crochet Hook No. 7.

Felt lining. A bone ring.

BODY . . . Starting at top with Turquoise, ch 68. **1st row:** Sc in 2nd ch from hook, * skip 2 ch, 5 dc in next ch (shell made), skip 2 ch, sc in next ch. Repeat from * across. Ch 3, turn. **2nd row:** * Sc in center dc of next shell, shell in back loop of next sc. Repeat from * across, ending with 3 dc in back loop of last sc (half shell made). Ch 1, turn. **3rd and 4th rows:** Sc in first dc, * shell in back loop of next sc, sc in center dc of next shell. Repeat from * across, ending with half shell in back loop of last sc. **5th row:**

continued on page 28

Shown in color on the back cover.

Owl

MATERIALS REQUIRED:
Art. 600 Lily Cotton Yarn Skeins **or**
Art. 930 Sugar 'N Cream Yarn Balls
2 skeins or balls Terra Cotta **and**
Art. 21 Lily Six Strand Floss
2 skeins Scarlet, 1 skein Brown and a scrap of Black.
Cochet Hooks Nos. 0 and 5.

FRONT—Body—With Terra Cotta and No. 0 hook, ch 20, sc in 4th ch from hook, (ch 1, sk 1 ch, sc in next ch) 8 times. **ROW 2**—Ch 3, turn, sc between 1st 2 sc, (ch 1, sc in next ch-1 sp) 8 times across to end ch-3. **ROW 3**—Ch 3, turn, sc in 1st ch-1 sp, (ch 1, sc in next ch-1 sp) repeated across to end ch-3, ch 1, hdc in same ch-3 (an increase). Repeat Row 3 once. **ROW 5**—Ch 3, turn, sc in 1st ch-1 sp, (ch 1, sc in next sp) repeated across to end ch-3. Repeat Row 3 twice, Row 5 once, Row 3 twice, Row 5 twice, Row 3 twice, Row 5 once (thru Row 15), then Row 5 six times more (thru Row 21). **ROW 22**—Ch 3, turn, draw up a lp in each of 1st 2 ch-1 sps, yarn over and draw thru all 3 lps on hook for a decrease, (ch 1, sc in next sp) repeated across to end ch-3. Repeat once. Repeat Row 5 six times (thru Row 29), Row 3 twice and Row 5 three times (thru Row 34). **ROW 35**—Ch 1, turn, in next ch-1 sp make 2 dc and 4 tr, dc and 2 hdc in next sp, (sc in next sp, sc in next sc) twice, hdc in next sp, hdc in next sc, (dc in next sp, dc in next sc) 4 times, dc in next sp, hdc in next sc, hdc in next sp, (sc in next sc, sc in next sp) twice, 2 hdc and dc in next sp, 4 tr and 2 dc in next sp, sc in end ch-3. Then work sc around Body to base of 1st ear, join and fasten off.

Tail—With Terra Cotta ch 8, sk 1 ch, sc in next 7 ch. Work following rows in back lps only. **ROW 2**—Ch 1, turn, sc in 7 sc. Repeat thru Row 20. Working across top with 1 st in end of each row, make a sc-decrease in 1st 2 rows, sk 1 row, hdc in next 2 rows, dc in next 10 rows, hdc in next 2 rows, sk 1 row, sc-decrease in 2 end rows. Fasten off. Working across bottom edge with Scarlet Floss and No. 5 hook, sc in 1st row, * ch 1, 3 long sc in center of next rib, inserting hook ½" down below edge, ch 1, sc between ribs. Repeat from * across to corner. Fasten off. Sew top of Tail to bottom of Body.

Branch—With Brown Floss ch 6, join with sl st to form ring. Ch 1, 2 sc, 2 hdc and 6 dc in ring. Working in back lps only make dc in 10 sts around and around without joining until skein is almost used up, hdc

continued on page 28

Shown in color on the inside front cover.

Penguin

MATERIALS:

J. & P. COATS "KNIT-CRO-SHEEN," **Art. A.64:** 2 balls of No. 12 Black and 1 ball of No. 1 White . . . A few yards of No. 10-A Canary Yellow and No. 43 Dk. Yellow . . . **Milwards Steel Crochet Hooks** No. 4 and No. 7 . . . A bone ring.

FRONT—Body . . . Starting at center with double strand of White and No. 4 hook, ch 30. **1st rnd:** 3 sc in 2nd ch from hook, sc in each ch across, 3 sc in last ch; working along opposite side of starting chain, make sc in each ch across. **2nd rnd:** Sc in each sc around, increasing 3 sc evenly on each end—*to inc 1 sc, make 2 sc in 1 sc.* Repeat 2nd rnd until piece measures 6 inches long. Break off.

SIDE PIECE . . . Mark off center sc at each end. Skip 4 sc from center sc. **1st row:** Attach double strand of Black to next sc and, picking up back loop of each sc, sc in each sc across to within 4 sc of center sc on opposite end. Ch 1, turn. **2nd to 7th rows incl:** Dec 1 sc—*to dec 1 sc, work off 2 sc as 1 sc*—sc in each sc across to within last 2 sc, dec 1 sc. Ch 1, turn. Break off. Complete other side to correspond.

RIGHT FLIPPER . . . Skip 18 free sc loops on last White row. **1st row:** Using No. 7 hook, attach a single strand of Black and, picking up free loop of each sc, sc in next 8 sc, 2 sc in next sc. Ch 1, turn. **2nd row:** 2 sc in first sc, sc in next 7 sc, dec 1 sc. Ch 1, turn. **3rd row:** Dec 1 sc, sc in next 7 sc, 2 sc in last sc. Ch 1, turn. **4th row:** Repeat 2nd row. **5th row:** Dec 2 sc, sc in next 5 sc, 2 sc in last sc. Ch 1, turn. **6th row:** Dec 1 sc, sc in next 3 sc, dec 2 sc. Ch 1, turn. **7th row:** Work off 3 sc as 1 sc. Break off. Make Left Flipper to correspond.

HEAD . . . Starting at center with double strand of Black and No. 4 hook, ch 2. **1st rnd:** 7 sc in 2nd ch from hook. **2nd rnd:** 2 sc in each sc around. **3rd rnd:** Sc in each sc, increasing 7 sc evenly around. Repeat 3rd rnd until piece measures 2¾ inches in diameter Break off.

EYE . . . Starting at center with a single strand of White and No. 7 hook, ch 2. **1st rnd:** 7 sc in 2nd ch from hook. **2nd rnd:** 2 sc in each sc around.

continued on page 48

OWL *(continued from page 27)*

in next 2 sts, sc in next 2 sts, sl st in next. Sew end tog. Sew across joining of Body and Tail.

Foot — With Red Floss (ch 10, sk 1 ch, sc in next 3 ch, hdc in next 5 ch, sc in next ch) 3 times. (Sc between toes, sc in next toe) twice across top. Fasten off. Make 2 pieces. Sew over Branch as illustrated.

Eye—With Terra Cotta ch 6, join with sl st to form ring. **ROW 1**—Ch 1, 10 sc in ring. Do not join rows but mark end of each row. **ROW 2**—Sc in front lp of 1st sc, (2 sc in front lp of next sc, sc in next sc) repeated around. **ROW 3**—Sc in remaining back lp of 1st sc in Row 1 behind last row, (2 sc in back lp of next sc in Row 1, sc in next sc) repeated around. **ROWS 4 and 5**—(Sc in both lps of next sc, 2 sc in next sc) repeated for 2 rows. **ROW 6**—(Sc in next 2 sc, 2 sc in next sc) repeated around, sl st in next sc. Fasten off. **Edge**—With Scarlet Floss and No. 5 hook, make a long sc over last row, inserting hook down between last 2 rows, (ch 2, a long sc over next sc) repeated around to within 1¼″ of start of row. Fasten off. Make a 2d Eye and sew tog. across 1¼″ gap in Edge Row.

Beak—With Terra Cotta ch 2, 5 sc in 2d ch from hook. Without joining and working in back lps only, make sc in 5 sc around and around for 1¾″. (A decrease in next 2 sc) 3 times. Sew end tog. Sew Beak between eyes with pointed end down. **Pupil**—With Black Floss ch 5, join with sl st to form ring. Ch 1, 8 sc in ring, join and fasten off. Make two. Sew one in center of each Eye. Sew Eyes on Head as illustrated.

BACK—Repeat Body thru Row 17. **ROW 18**—Ch 3, turn, sc in next ch-1 sp, (ch 1, sc in next sp) twice, ch 9, sk 4 sps, sc in next sp, complete row in pattern. **ROW 19**—Ch 3, turn, sc in 1st ch-1 sp, (ch 1, sc in next sc) 8 times, ch 1, sc in 1st st of ch-9, (ch 1, sk 1 ch, sc in next ch) 4 times, (ch 1, sc in next ch-1 sp) 3 times. Repeat Row 5 twice (thru Row 21). Repeat from Row 22 to end.

Thumb—With Terra Cotta follow directions on Page 5. Repeat Tail except omit Scarlet Edge. Sew to Body. Sew Front and Back tog. leaving top of head open. Cover a bone ring with sc in Terra Cotta and sew to Back 1″ below top. Steam and press dry on back thru a cloth. ✿

CHICKEN *(continued from page 26)*

Sc in first dc, * shell in back loop of next sc, sc in center dc of next shell. Repeat from * across, ending with sc in center dc of last shell. Ch 3, turn. **6th to 9th rows incl:** Repeat 2nd to 5th rows incl. **10th row:** * Sc in center dc of next shell, shell in back loop of next sc. Repeat from * across, ending with 2 dc in back loop of last sc. Ch 1, turn. **11th row:** Sc in first dc, * shell in back loop of next sc, sc in center dc of next shell. Repeat from * across, ending with sc in last shell. Ch 3, turn. **12th row:** * Sc in center dc of next shell, shell in back loop of next sc. Repeat from * across, ending with sc in center dc of last shell. Ch 3, turn. **13th row:** Dc in first sc, * sc in center dc of next shell, shell in back loop of next sc. Repeat from * across, ending with sc in last shell. Ch 3, turn. **14th row:** * Sc in center dc of next shell, shell in back loop of next sc. Repeat from * across, ending with sc in top of turning chain. Ch 3, turn. **15th, 16th and 17th rows:** * Sc in center dc of next shell, shell in back loop of next sc. Repeat from * across, ending with sc in center dc of last shell. Ch 3, turn. Break off at end of 17th row. Attach Turquoise to first sc on first row and, working over rounded end, sc closely across to opposite end of first row. Break off. **Next row:** Attach Purple to first sc on rounded end of body, ch 2, half dc in next 9 sc, dc in next 24 sc, half dc in next 3 sc, sc in next 3 sc. Break off. **Following row:** Attach Black to first half dc, sc in same half dc and in each Purple st across, sc in next 5 Turquoise sc. Break off.

HEAD . . . Starting at center with Turquoise, ch 5. Join with sl st to form ring. **1st rnd:** Ch 3, 14 dc in ring. Join with sl st to top of ch-3. Ch 3, turn. **2nd rnd:** Dc in same place as sl st, 2 dc in each dc around. Join. Ch 3, turn. **3rd rnd:** Dc in same place as sl st, * dc in next dc, 2 dc in next dc. Repeat from * around. Join and turn (45 dc). **4th rnd:** Sc in same place as sl st, sc in next 34 dc, half dc in same place as last sc, half dc in next dc, dc in next 9 dc, sl st in first sc. Ch 4, turn.

To Shape Neck: 1st row: Tr in first dc, tr in next dc, dc in next dc, half dc in next dc, sc in next 7 sts. Ch 3, turn. **2nd row:** Skip first sc, dc in next 5 sc, tr in next 5 sts and in top of turning chain. Ch 4, turn. **3rd row:** Make tr and dc in first tr, dc in next 2 sts, half dc in next 4 sts, sc in each remaining st and in top of turning chain. Break off (long side is back of neck).

COMB . . . 1st row: Skip 3 sc on Head from back of neck. Attach Spanish Red to next sc, 2 sc in same sc, sc in next sc, half dc in next sc, (dc in next sc, 2 dc in next sc) 6 times. Ch 2, turn. **2nd row:** 2 sc in 2nd ch from hook, skip first dc, sc in next dc, * ch 2, 2 sc in 2nd ch from hook, skip next st, sc in next st. Repeat from * across Comb. Break off.

BEAK . . . 1st row: Leaving 8 sc free following Comb, attach Black to next sc. Ch 3, dc in next 3 sc. Ch 3, turn. **2nd row:** Skip first dc, holding back on hook the last loop of each dc make dc in next 2 dc, thread over and draw through all loops on hook (cluster made), dc in top of starting chain. Ch 3, turn. **3rd row:** Skip first dc, make a cluster over next dc and in top of turning chain. Break off.

Sew Head to Body.

EYE . . . With Black, ch 2, 10 sc in 2nd ch from hook. Join and break off. Sew in place.

WING . . . Starting at pointed end with Purple, ch 4. **1st row:** 2 dc in 4th ch from hook. Ch 3, turn. **2nd row:** Dc in first dc, 3 dc in next dc, 2 dc in top of starting chain. Ch 3, turn. **3rd to 6th rows incl:** Skip first dc, dc in each dc across, making 3 dc in center dc of 3 dc group, dc in top of turning chain. Ch 3, turn. **7th, 8th and 9th rows:** Skip first dc, dc in each dc across, dc in top of turning chain. Ch 3, turn. **10th and 11th rows:** Skip first dc, work off next 3 dc as 1 dc, dc in each dc across to within last 2 dc and turning chain; work off last 3 dc as 1 dc. Ch 3, turn. Ch 1 to turn at end of 11th row. **12th row:** Work off first 2 sc as 1 sc, sc in each dc across to within last 2 dc, work off last 2 sc as 1 sc. Break off.

TRIM . . . With Black (ch 16, sc in 2nd ch from hook and in each ch across) 3 times. Break off. Sew to Wing and sew Wing in place.

Trace outline of chicken on felt. Cut felt slightly smaller than pot holder. Sew in place. Make another Body, Head and Wing the same way. Join pieces by sewing across top of back, around head and down 2 inches of front. With Turquoise, sc closely around bone ring. Join and break off. Sew to back. ✿

Duck

This holder may be made with any of the American Thread Company products listed below:

Material	Quantity	Size of Needle
"STAR" Cotton Yarn Article 75	1 Skein Each Green, White and Red	Steel 00
or		
"STAR" Rug Yarn Article 44	2 Skeins White 1 Skein Each Green and Red	Steel 00
and		
"STAR" Six Strand Embroidery Cotton Article 50	2 Skeins Yellow 1 Skein Black	Steel 8

FRONT: With Green ch 2, 6 s c in 2nd st from hook, do not join this or the following 3 rows, place a marker at beginning of each of the next 3 rows.
2nd Row. 2 s c in each s c.
3rd Row. Working in s c, increase in every other st.
4th Row. Increase in every 3rd st.
5th Row. Increase in every 4th s c (30 s c) ch 1, turn.
6th Row. 1 s c in each of the next 6 sts, ch 1, turn.
7th Row. 1 s c in each of the next 3 s c, break Green, attach White (when changing Color always complete last half of st with next Color) and work 1 s c in each of the next 2 s c, 2 s c in next s c, ch 1, turn.
8th Row. 2 s c in each of the next 3 s c, 1 s c in next s c, drop White (always drop Colors to wrong side of work), attach Red and work 2 s c in each of the next 2 s c, ch 1, turn.
9th Row. 2 s c in next s c, 1 s c in each of the next 2 s c, drop Red, pick up White and work 1 s c in each of the next 5 s c, 2 s c in each of the next 3 s c, ch 1, turn.
10th Row. 1 s c in each of the next 12 s c, with Red 1 s c in each of the next 3 s c, ch 3, turn (counts as 1 d c in each row).
11th Row. 2 d c in each of the next 2 sts, 1 d c in each of the next 2 sts, 1 s c in each of the next 3 sts, with White 1 s c in each of the next 7 s c, ch 1, turn.
12th Row. 2 s c in next s c, 1 s c in each of the next 7 s c, with Red 1 s c in each of the next 3 sts, 1 d c in each of the next 6 sts, ch 3, turn.
13th Row. 2 d c in next st, 1 d c in each of the next 3 sts, 1 s c in each of the next 2 sts, with White 1 s c in each of the next 9 sts, 2 s c in each of the next 2 sts, ch 1, turn.
14th Row. 1 s c in each of the next 14 s c, with Red 1 d c in each of the next 4 sts, 2 d c in each of the next 3 sts, ch 3, turn.
15th Row. 1 d c in each of the next 3 sts, 1 s c in each of the next 3 sts, with White 1 s c in each of the next 17 sts, ch 1, turn.
16th Row. 2 s c in next s c, 1 s c in each of the next 18 s c, with Red 1 s c in each of the next 3 s c, 2 s c in next st, 1 s c in next st, ch 1, turn.
17th Row. 1 s c in each of the next 4 sts, with White 1 s c in each of the next 22 sts, ch 1, turn.
18th Row. 2 s c in next s c, 1 s c in each of the next 23 s c, with Red 1 s c in next s c, 2 s c in next s c, ch 1, turn.
19th Row. S c in next s c, break Red, with White 1 s c in each remaining s c, ch 1, turn.
20th Row. 1 s c in each s c decreasing 1 s c at end of row (to decrease: * insert hook in next st, pull loop through, repeat from * once, yarn over and pull through all loops at one time), ch 3, turn.
21st Row. 1 d c in each of the next 5 sts, 1 s c in each remaining st, ch 1 to turn each of the following rows.
Next 9 Rows. Work even in s c.

31st Row. Repeat 20th row.
Next 4 Rows. Decrease 1 s c at beginning and end of each row.
36th Row. Decrease 2 s c at end of row.
37th Row. Increase 1 s c at end of row.
38th Row. Increase 1 s c at beginning of row and decrease 1 s c at end of row.
39th Row. Decrease 2 s c at beginning of row and increase 1 s c at end of row.
40th Row. Increase 1 s c at beginning of row, decrease 2 s c at end of row.
41st Row. Repeat 39th row.
42nd Row. 1 sl st in each s c, break yarn.
BEAK: With Yellow ch 16, s c in 2nd st from hook, 1 s c in each remaining st of ch, ch 1, turn.
2nd Row. Increase 1 s c at beginning and end of row, ch 1, turn.
3rd Row. Decrease 1 s c at end of row, ch 1, turn.
4th Row. Decrease 1 s c at beginning of row, ch 1, turn.
5th Row. Repeat 3rd row.
6th Row. 2 s c in next s c, 1 s c in each of the next 10 s c, ch 4, turn.
7th Row. 2 s c in 2nd st from hook, 1 s c in each of the next 2 sts of ch, 1 s c in each remaining s c increasing 1 s c at end of row.
8th Row. Repeat 2nd row, break thread.
Work another section in same manner.
BACK SECTION: Work 1st 17 rows of front section.
18th Row. 2 s c in next s c, 1 s c in each of the next 3 s c, ch 9, skip 9 s c (thumb opening), 1 s c in each of the next 11 s c, with Red 1 s c in next s c, 2 s c in next s c, ch 1, turn.
19th Row. S c in next s c, break Red, with White 1 s c in each s c and 1 s c in each st of ch, ch 1, turn and complete back same as front section.
THUMB: With White follow directions given for thumb on page 5.
FOOT: With Yellow ch 10, s c in 2nd st from hook, 1 s c in next st of ch, ch 3, s c in 2nd st from hook, 2 s c in next st of ch, 1 s c in each of the next 7 sts of ch, ch 1, turn.
2nd Row. Sl st in each of the next 3 s c, 1 s c in each of the next 4 s c, sl st in each of the next 3 sts, break thread. Work another section in same manner. Sew sections together and sew to duck as illustrated. Sew beak in position on front and back sections. With Black "STAR" Six Strand Embroidery Cotton using 12 strands, embroider eye and lines as illustrated. Sew back and front sections together leaving 14 rows of breast free for opening.
With White cover a bone ring with s c and attach to back of holder about 1 inch down from top. ✿

Cats on-a-Rack

MATERIALS: Clark's O.N.T. Cotton Rug Yarn, *1 ball each of Dark Yellow and Red . . . Steel Crochet Hook Size G . . . A 7-inch piece of wood, 3/4 inch in diameter . . . 2 brass hooks . . . 3 brass rings.*

CAT POTHOLDER—Body . . . Starting at center with Red, ch 2. **1st rnd:** 6 sc in 2nd ch from hook. **2nd rnd:** 2 sc in each sc around (12 sc). **3rd rnd:** * 2 sc in next sc (1 sc increased), sc in next sc. Repeat from * around. Continue making sc in each sc around, increasing as necessary to keep work flat—*to inc 1 sc, make 2 sc in 1 sc.* Do not break off.

TAIL . . . Ch 6, sc in 2nd ch from hook, skip 1 ch, sc in next ch, dc in next 2 ch, skip 2 sc on Body, sl st in next sc. Break off.

HEAD . . . With Red, work 5 rnds of sc as for Body. Do not break off.

EARS . . . Ch 4, sc in 2nd ch from hook, dc in next ch, tr in next ch, skip 2 sc on Head, sc in next 3 sc, ch 4 and make opposite Ear to correspond, sl st in next sc. Break off. This completes one side of pot holder. Make other side same as this, using Yellow and making Tail to correspond. Sew both sides together. Sew ring at top. Make another pot holder same as this.

BAR COVER . . . With Red, ch 9. **1st row:** Sc in 2nd ch from hook, sc in next 7 ch. Ch 1, turn. **2nd row:** Sc in each sc across. Ch 1, turn. Repeat 2nd row until piece measures 7 inches. Break off. Cover wooden bar with this piece and sew edges neatly.

HANGER . . . With Yellow, ch 4. **1st row:** Sc in 2nd ch from hook and in next 2 ch. Ch 1, turn. **2nd row:** Sc in next 3 sc. Ch 1, turn. Repeat 2nd row until piece measures 10 inches. Break off. Sew ends of hanger to ends of bar.

CAT ORNAMENT (Make one Red and one Yellow)—Body . . . Work 4 rnds of sc as for Head. Do not break off.

TAIL . . . Ch 4, sc in 2nd ch from hook, skip 1 ch, sc in next ch, skip 1 sc of Body, sl st in next sc. Break off.

HEAD . . . Work as for first 3 rnds of Body but do not break off.

EARS . . . Ch 3, sc in 2nd ch from hook, dc in next ch, skip 1 sc of Head, sc in next sc, ch 3 and complete other ear to correspond, sl st in next sc. Break off. Sew Yellow and Red sides together, inserting 3 strands of Yellow between sides for whiskers. Stiffen whiskers with clear nail polish and turn up. Screw hooks in place. Sew ring to top of ornament. Sew ornament at top of hanger.

Scottie in Puff Stitch

One of the most novel pot holders to be crocheted that we have ever seen! Firm and heavy for use with hottest pots and pans, — a dressy, ornamental holder to hang beside the stove. It's double — to slip over the handle!

MATERIALS: 100 yds. White Enterprise Yarn and just a few yards of color (for eye and collar) will be needed for the holders. The Sleepy Time Scottie will need 60 to 75 yards more, of White, for the inset piece. Steel Crochet Hook No. 1.

NOTE: Puff Stitch is a new stitch—there are new abbreviations not commonly used in crocheting, in these instructions:—for increases (inc.) make 1 sc, 1 dc in first st, to start puff row; 1 dc, 1 sc, in last st to end a puff row. Also PUFF STITCH OR PUFFS are indicated as PS.

Two sides will be needed for either the holders or the toy.

Starting at feet, with White ch 8, 7 sc on chain.

ROW 2: Ch 1, turn, sc in last sc, * 2 dc in next sc, holding final loop of each dc on hook, thread over and pull through all three loops at once. (1 puff st (PS) made), sc in next sc, (pull it down tight, to let the ps puff out on back of work) which will be the right side. Repeat from * across (3 Ps).

ROW 3: Ch 1, turn, sc in first sc, (sc in ps, sc in next sc), repeat across (7 sc). Repeat Row 2.

ROW 5: Ch 1, turn, sc in first 6 sts, 2 sc in end sc.

ROW 6: Ch 1, turn, sc, dc, (an inc.), in first sc, sc in next sc, ps in next, repeat to end (3 ps and 1 inc.).

ROW 7: Ch 1, turn, sc in each st (9 sc). Repeat Row 2, (4 ps). Break thread and make second piece to correspond, working inc. at beginning of sc rows with ch 2, turn, sc in second st from hook, sc in each st across. Then work puff row to within 1 st of end, inc. in end st. Repeat last 2 rows of first foot (making inc. as before at opposite ends of row) then ch 7, sl st to first sc in puff Row 8 of first foot. Cut thread 2" from work.

BODY: With right side up, attach thread to first sc of first foot, ch 1, sc in each st across, working over ends, covering them up (25 sc in row).

ROW 2: Ch 1, turn, ps across (12 ps). Repeat Rows 1 and 2 twice.

ROW 7: Ch 1, turn, sc in first 23 sts.

ROW 8: Ch 1, turn, work 11 ps in row. Repeat Row 7 (21 sc), then Row 8 (10 ps).

ROW 11: Ch 2, turn, sk 1 st of 2-ch, sc in next 22 sts across.

ROW 12: Ch 1, turn, 10 ps across, inc. in end sc.

TAIL: Ch 1, turn, sc in first 9 sts, ch 1, turn, 4 ps in row. Ch 2, sk 1 st of 2-ch, sc in next 8 sts. Ch 1, turn, 3 ps to end, inc. in end st. Ch 1, turn, sc in first 7 sts. Ch 1, turn, sk 2 sc (sc in next, ps in next) repeat once, sc in end st. Ch 1, turn, sc in first 5 sts. Fasten off.

HEAD: Ch 12, 11 sc on ch. Ch 1, turn, 5 ps across. Ch 1, turn, sc in each 11 sts across. Ch 1, turn, 5 ps in row. Ch 1, turn, sc in each 11 sts. Ch 1, turn, 5 ps in row. Ch 1, turn, sc in each st to end. 2 sc in end st (12 sc). Ch 1, turn, inc. in first sc, (sc in next, ps in next) repeat across (5 ps and 1 inc.). Ch 1, turn, sc in each st to end, 2 sc in end st (14 sc). Ch 1, turn, inc. in first sc, sc in next, ps in next, sc in next, holding 2 loops of last sc on hook, drop White on wrong side, draw loop of color through 2 loops on hook, completing sc, work over starting end of color and White, carrying it along, make 1 ps in color (for eye), pick up White, draw through 2 loops of final sc, fasten off color, and complete row of puffs in White. Ch 1, turn, sc in each st to end, 2 sc in end sc (15 sc). Ch 1, turn, inc. in first sc, work in ps to end of row. Ch 1, turn, sc in 17 sts. Ch 1, turn, 7 ps in row. Ch 1, turn, sc in each st across. Fasten off.

Sew head to body as illustrated. Make second side to correspond, BUT BE SURE TO MAKE INCREASES AND DECREASES AT OPPOSITE ENDS OF EACH ROW, so that when wrong sides of work are placed in position to sew together, they will be alike and same size.

FOR HOLDER: Pad each half, then line with muslin. Press each piece on wrong side. Place padded sides together, starting at base of neck and stitch together around nose, head, and across top of body and around to base of tail.

COLLAR: With color, ch 26, 25 sc on ch. Cut thread 6" from work, thread to needle, place around neck and sew ends together. Sew bone ring to collar as illustrated. ✿

Cats 'n' Dogs

Not raining! but cute Hot Pot Holders that will attract attention and be serviceable too. They are to be padded and lined to cover the joining of the head and body, for added protection.

MATERIALS: A ball of White Enterprise Yarn and 30 yds. of color for a pair.

CAT—BODY: With White, ch 25, sc in second st from hook, (ch 1, sk 1, sc in next) twice, hdc in 2 sts, dc in 2, sk 1, sc in 3, sk 1, hdc, dc in 2, hdc, sk 1, sc, ch 1, sk 1, sc in next, ch 1, 2 sc in end st.

ROW 2: Ch 2, sc in last sc, (ch 1, sc in next) 3 times, (ch 1, sk 1, sc in next) 7 times, ch 1, 2 sc in end.

NOTE: The abbreviation ptn or ptna = pattern or

continued on next page

 (continued from page 31)

pattern across mentioned in following rows means (ch 1, sc in next sc) to be worked between increases or decreases at end of rows. Turn to start each succeeding row.

ROW 3: Ch 2, sc in last sc, ptna, with 2 sc in end. Repeat this row 3 times.

ROW 7: Ch 1, sc in last sc, ptna. Repeat 4 times.

ROW 12: Ch 1, sc in last 2 sc, ptna to second from end, sc in end.

ROW 13: Ch 1, sk last sc, sc in next, ptn to second sc from end, sl st in end. Repeat Rows 7 and 13.

ROW 16: Ch 1, 2 sc in last sc, ptn to end, 2 sc in end. Repeat Rows 12, 13, 7 and 13. Fasten off.

EDGE: Work around (except across top) as Edge on Dog.

HEAD: With White, ch 14, 2 sc in second st from hook, ch 1, sk 1, sc in next, hdc in 2, dc in 3, holding last loop of each on hook, thread over and pull through all 4 loops at once (a cluster), hdc in 2, sc, ch 1, 2 sc in end st.

ROW 2: Ch 2, 2 sc in last sc, (ch 1, sc in next) twice, (ch 1, sc in next second st) 3 times. Ch 1, sc in next, ch 1, 2 sc in end.

ROW 3: Ch 2, sc in last sc, ptna.

ROW 4: Ch 1, 2 sc in last sc, ptna, 2 sc in end.

ROW 5: Ch 1, sc in last sc, ptna. Repeat 3 times.

ROW 9: Ch 1, sk last sc, sc in next, ptn 9 times, sl st in end sc. Repeat Row 4 once; Row 5 three times; and Row 4 once.

ROW 15: Ch 3, dc in last sc, 2 dc and 1 hdc in next, hdc in next, sl st in next, ch 1, sc in next, 2 hdc in next (2 dc in next) twice, 2 hdc in next, sc in next, ch 1, sl st in next, hdc in next, hdc and 2 dc in next, (dc, ch 3 and sl st) in end sc. Fasten off. Work around Edge in Color. Ch 2, sl st in same dc at top of each Ear.

BOW: With Color, ch 2, sc in first st. Ch 1, turn, 2 sc in sc. (Ch 1, turn, sc in each sc, with 2 sc in end) for 4 rows. (Ch 1, turn, 6 sc) twice. Fasten off. Make four pieces. Sew these on top of Body, half the width of 2 upper pieces extending above Body, then lap Head slightly over top edge of Bow and Body and tack. With strand of Color, embroider Eyes and Whiskers on Head, Legs and Body, as in illustration. Pad and line, and sew ring at top.

DOG: Starting at bottom of body—With White ch 27, sc in second st from hook, ch 1, sc in next second st, 2 hdc, 4 dc, sk 1, 4 sc, sk 1, 2 hdc, 5 dc, sk 1, sc, ch 1, sk 1, 2 sc in end st.

ROW 2: Ch 1, 2 sc in last sc, (ch 1, sc in next) twice, (ch 1, sk 1, sc in next) 9 times, ch 1, 2 sc in end sc.

See note in Cat Instructions, Row 2.

ROW 3: Ch 1, sc in last sc, ptna 14 times.

ROW 4: Ch 2, sk last sc, sc in next, ptna to second sc from end, sc in end.

ROW 5: Ch 1, sc in last sc, ptna, 2 sc in end. Repeat this row once.

ROW 7: Ch 1, sc in last sc, ptna. Repeat Row 7, then 5.

ROW 10: Ch 1, sc in last 2 sc, ptna.

ROW 11: Ch 1, sc in last sc, ptna to second sc from end, sc in end sc.

ROW 12: Ch 1, sc in last 2 sc, ptna. Repeat Rows 11 and 12.

ROW 15: Ch 1, sk last sc, sc in next, * ptna to second sc from end, sl st in end.

ROW 16: Ch 2, sk sl st, sc in next 2 sc, repeat from * in Row 15.

ROW 17: Ch 1, sk sl st, 2 sc in next sc, ptna 11 times, sc in next, sl st in end. Repeat Row 12; Row 7 four times; Rows 11 and 4 once.

ROW 25: Ch 1, sk last sc, sc in next, ptna. Repeat Row 4.

ROW 27: Ch 1, 2 sc in last sc, sc in next, ptn 8 times, sc in end sc. Repeat Row 11 once; Row 7 twice.

ROW 31: Ch 1, 2 sc in last sc, ptna, 2 sc in end. Repeat Rows 7, 5, 12 and 4.

ROW 36: Ch 1, sc in last sc, ptna to second sc from end, sl st in end.

ROW 37: Ch 2, sk sl st, sl st in next sc, ch 1, (2 hdc in next) twice, sc in next sc, 2 hdc in next, 2 dc in next, 2 hdc in next, sc in next, in ptn 4 times, sc in end.

ROW 38: Ch 1, sk last sc, sc in next, ch 1, 2 hdc in next, 2 dc in next, 2 dc and 1 hdc in next, ch 1, sl st in next sc. Fasten off.

EDGE: Join Color, (ch 1, sl st in next second row or st) around. Fasten off.

LEFT EAR: With Color, ch 2, 2 sc in starting st, ch 1, sc in last sc, 2 sc in next, * (ch 1, sc in each sc with 2 sc in end sc) twice. Ch 1, sc in each sc twice. Ch 1, sk last sc, sc in 4 sc. Ch 3, dc and hdc in last sc, sc in next, sl st in next. Fasten off.

RIGHT EAR: Repeat Left Ear to *. (Ch 1, sc in each sc. Ch 1, sc in each sc across, with 2 sc in end sc) twice. Ch 1, sk 1, sc in 4 sc. Ch 1, 3 sc and sl st. Ch 1, sl st in next sc, sc in next, 2 sc in next, ch 6, sk last ch st, 2 sc in next, sc in next 3 ch sts, sl st in next sc. Fasten off.

EYES: With Color, ch 2, 5 sc in starting st, sl st in first sc. Fasten off. Make 2.

NOSE: With Color, ch 2, (sc, hdc, 3 dc, hdc and sc) in first st. Fasten off.

Sew Ears, Eyes and Nose in place. Following illustrations and using a single strand, embroider Head and Legs, using 1/4" to 1/2" back stitches. With White make a tiny stitch on right half of each Eye for highlight.

Western Boot

This holder may be made with any of the American Thread Company products listed below:

Material	Quantity	Size of Needle
"STAR" Cotton Yarn Article 75	1 Skein Each Black and White	Steel 00
or		
"STAR" Rug Yarn Article 44	1 Skein Each Black and White	Steel 00
or		
"AUNT LYDIA" Heavy Rug Yarn Article 235	1 Skein Each Black and White	Bone 6
and		
"STAR" Six Strand Embroidery Cotton Article 50	1 Skein Each Red, Green and Blue	Steel 4

Directions are given for "STAR" Cotton Yarn and "STAR" Rug Yarn. *"AUNT LYDIA" Heavy Rug Yarn is given in parenthesis.*

LOWER SECTION: With Black ch 5 (5), s c in 2nd st from hook, 1 s c in each remaining st of ch, ch 1 to turn all rows.

2nd Row. Working in s c, increase 1 s c in last s c. Work 2 (1) rows even in s c.

5th (4th) Row. 2 s c in 1st (last) s c, 1 s c in each remaining s c.

Work 2 (1) rows even.

8th (6th) Row. Same as 2nd row.

9th (7th) Row. Same as 5th row (work even).

10th (8th) Row. Same as 2nd row.

11th (9th) Row. 2 s c in 1st s c, 1 s c in each of the next 6 (5) s c, decrease 1 s c (to decrease: insert hook in st, pull loop through, insert in next st, pull loop through, yarn over and work all loops at one time). Work 1 (1) row even, ch 5 (4), turn.

13th (11th) Row. 1 s c in 2nd st from hook, 1 s c in each of the next 3 (2) sts of ch, 1 s c in each of the next 7 (6) s c, decrease 1 s c.

14th (12th) Row. 1 s c in each of the 1st 10 (8) s c, sl st in next st.

15th (13th) Row. Skip the sl st, 2 s c in next s c, 1 s c in each remaining s c.

16th (14th) Row. 1 s c in each of the 1st 8 (7) s c.

17th (15th) Row. Decrease 1 st, 1 s c in each remaining s c. Work 8 (6) rows even.

26th (22nd) Row. Decrease 1 st, 1 s c in each of the next 4 s c, 2 s c in next s c, do not turn.

HEEL: Working along side of work insert hook in same space, pull loop through, insert hook in next row, pull loop through, yarn over and work off all loops at one time, 1 s c in each of the next 8 (6) rows.

2nd Row. 2 s c in 1st s c, 1 s c in each of the next 6 (5) s c, decrease 1 s c.

3rd Row. Decrease 1 s c, 1 s c in each of the next 6 (4) s c, 2 s c in next s c.

4th Row. 1 s c in each s c, decreasing 1 s c at end of row, break yarn.

Work another section in same manner.

UPPER SECTION: With White ch 15 (14), 1 s c in 2nd st from hook, 1 s c in each remaining st of ch.

2nd and 3rd Rows. 1 s c in each s c.

4th Row. Increase 1 s c at beginning and end of row.

5th Row. Increase 1 s c at end of row.

Work 3 (1) rows even.

9th and 10th (7th and 8th) Rows. Same as 5th row. Work 2 rows even (omit).

13th and 14th (9th and 10th) Rows. Same as 5th row. Work 1 row even.

16th (12th) Row. 2 s c in 1st s c, 1 s c in each of the next 18 (17) s c, decrease in next 2 sts.

17th (13th) Row. Decrease 1 st, 1 s c in each remaining s c.

18th (14th) Row. Skip 1 st, 1 s c in each of the next 15 (14) s c, decrease 1 st, sl st in next st, break yarn.

Work another section in same manner as far as the 9th (9th) row.

10th Row. 1 s c in each of the 1st 7 (5) s c, ch 8 (6), skip 8 (6) s c (thumb opening), 1 s c in next 2 (5) s c, 2 s c in last s c.

11th Row. 1 s c in each s c and 1 s c in each st of ch.

Continue working in same manner as 1st section.

THUMB: With White follow directions given for thumb on Page 5.

FINISHING: Sew each lower section to each upper section as illustrated. Then overcast each side together using White yarn on White and Black yarn on Black. With Black embroider a line in the center of the White section in outline st. Attach Black at back seam and work a row of s c all around top, join, ch 1, turn.

2nd Row. 1 s c in each s c, join, ch 1, turn. Repeat the last row once, break yarn.

With Green "STAR" Six Strand Embroidery Cotton ch 4, 1 s c in 2nd st from hook, 1 s c in each remaining st of ch, ch 1 to turn all rows.

2nd and 3rd Rows. 1 s c in each s c, break thread. Work 1 more Green diamond and 2 more Blue diamonds in same manner.

With Red ch 5, 1 s c in 2nd st from hook, 1 s c in each remaining st of ch, ch 1, turn.

2nd Row. 1 s c in each s c, ch 1, turn. Repeat last row twice, without breaking thread repeat from the 1st to 4th row in same manner, break thread. Applique trim to top of boot as follows: 1 Blue diamond, 2 Red, 1 Green, 1 Blue, 2 Red, and 1 Green as illustrated.

TASSEL: Over a 2 inch cardboard wind Red 10 times, cut one end, tie in center, then tie about ¼ inch down from top. Fasten to boot as illustrated.

STRAP: With Black ch 3 (3), s c in 2nd st from hook, 1 s c in next st of ch, ch 1 to turn all rows.

2nd Row. 1 s c in each s c. Repeat last row 7 (5) times.

10th (8th) Row. Decrease 1 s c, break yarn.

SPUR: With Black ch 4 (3), d c (s c) in 4th (3rd) st from hook, ch 3, sl st in top of d c (s c) for picot, * 2 d c (s c) in same st of ch, picot, repeat from * 3 times, join, break yarn leaving an end long enough to fasten to strap. Sew strap in position.

With Black cover a bone ring with s c and fasten to back of boot.

Bumble Bee

Shown in color on the front cover.

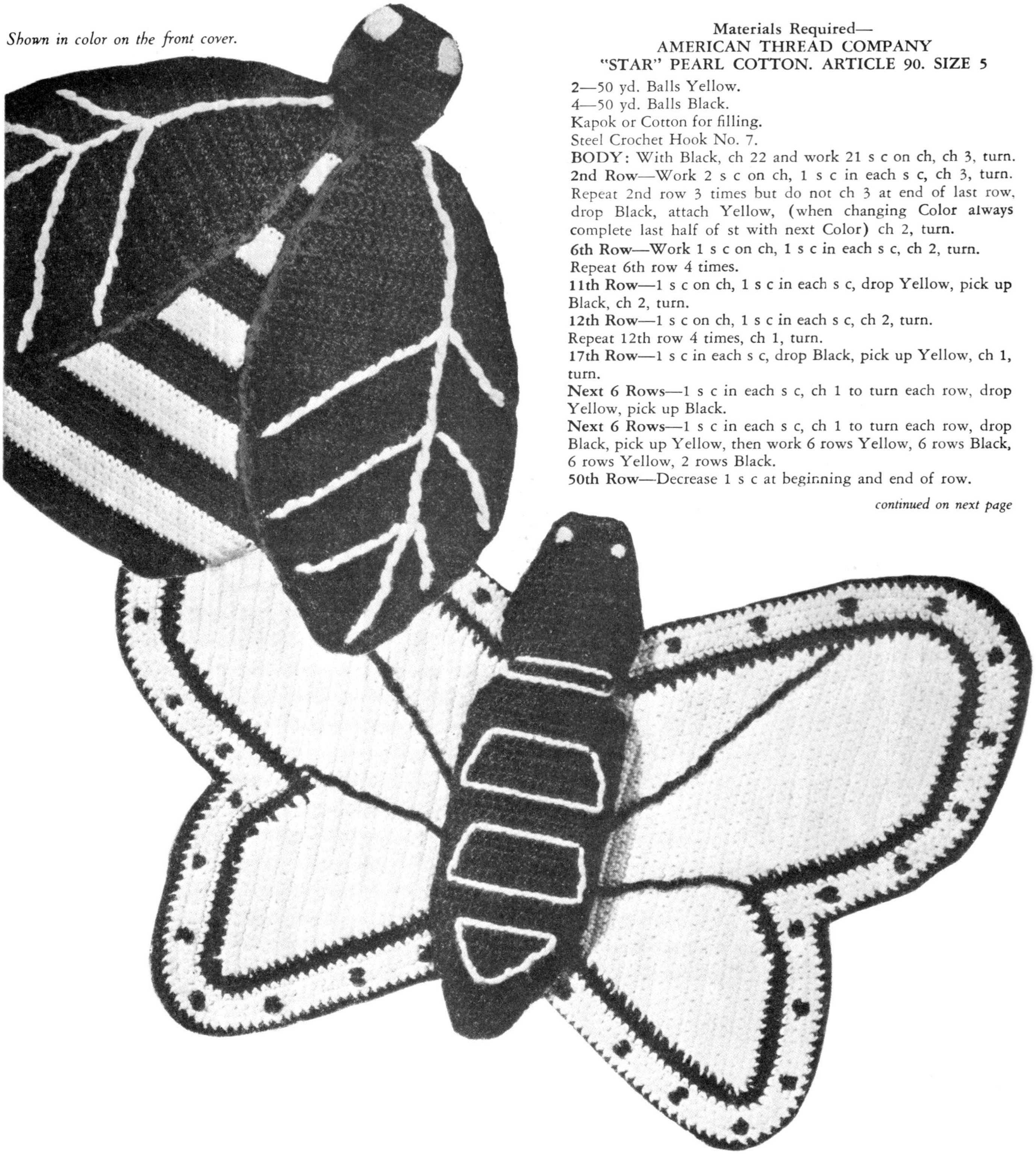

Materials Required—
AMERICAN THREAD COMPANY
"STAR" PEARL COTTON. ARTICLE 90. SIZE 5

2—50 yd. Balls Yellow.
4—50 yd. Balls Black.
Kapok or Cotton for filling.
Steel Crochet Hook No. 7.

BODY: With Black, ch 22 and work 21 s c on ch, ch 3, turn.

2nd Row—Work 2 s c on ch, 1 s c in each s c, ch 3, turn. Repeat 2nd row 3 times but do not ch 3 at end of last row, drop Black, attach Yellow, (when changing Color always complete last half of st with next Color) ch 2, turn.

6th Row—Work 1 s c on ch, 1 s c in each s c, ch 2, turn. Repeat 6th row 4 times.

11th Row—1 s c on ch, 1 s c in each s c, drop Yellow, pick up Black, ch 2, turn.

12th Row—1 s c on ch, 1 s c in each s c, ch 2, turn. Repeat 12th row 4 times, ch 1, turn.

17th Row—1 s c in each s c, drop Black, pick up Yellow, ch 1, turn.

Next 6 Rows—1 s c in each s c, ch 1 to turn each row, drop Yellow, pick up Black.

Next 6 Rows—1 s c in each s c, ch 1 to turn each row, drop Black, pick up Yellow, then work 6 rows Yellow, 6 rows Black, 6 rows Yellow, 2 rows Black.

50th Row—Decrease 1 s c at beginning and end of row.

continued on next page

BUMBLE BEE *(continued)*

51st Row—Work even in s c.
Repeat last 2 rows once, drop Black, pick up Yellow.
54th Row—Decrease 1 s c at beginning and end of row.
55th Row—Work even in s c, then repeat last 2 rows twice, drop Yellow, pick up Black.
60th Row—Decrease 1 s c at beginning and end of row.
Repeat last row 5 times, break thread.
Work another section in same manner. Sew 2 sections together leaving an opening for filling. Fill slightly with cotton and sew remainder of sections together.
WING: With Black, ch 7, 3 tr c in 5th st from hook, 1 tr c in next st of ch, 3 tr c in last st of ch, ch 4, turn.
2nd Row—2 d c in 4th ch from hook, 1 d c in each of the next 6 tr c, 2 d c in next tr c, ch 4, turn.
3rd Row—2 d c in 4th ch from hook, 1 d c in each d c working 2 d c in last d c, ch 4, turn.
Repeat 3rd row 5 times but ch 3 at end of 8th row to turn.
9th Row—1 d c in each d c, ch 3, turn.
Next 7 Rows—Repeat 9th row.
17th Row—Decrease 1 d c at beginning and end of row (decrease: thread over, insert in st, pull through and work off 2 loops, thread over, insert in next st, pull through and work off 2 loops, thread over and work off all loops at one time).
18th Row—1 d c in each d c, ch 3, turn.
Repeat last 2 rows twice, then repeat 17th row 7 times, ch 3, turn.
Next Row—Thread over, insert in st, pull through and work off 2 loops, * thread over, insert in next st, pull through and work off 2 loops, repeat from * across row, thread over and work off all loops at one time (top of wing), break thread.
Work another section in same manner. With double strand of Yellow, embroider top of wing as illustrated using outline st. With Black, crochet the 2 wing sections together with a row of s c.
Work another wing in same manner. With matching Colors, sew body sections together leaving an opening for filling. Fill slightly with cotton. Applique wing sections to top of body.
HEAD: With Black, ch 14 and work 13 s c on ch, ch 1, turn.
2nd Row—1 s c in each s c, ch 1, turn.
Repeat 2nd row 7 times.
10th Row—1 s c in each s c decreasing 1st and last st, ch 1, turn.
11th Row—Repeat 2nd row.
Repeat last 2 rows once, then repeat 7th row once, break thread. Work another head section in same manner. With double strand of Yellow embroider eyes in satin st. Sew head sections together leaving an opening for filling. Fill with cotton and sew remainder of sections together. Sew head section to body. With Black cover a bone ring with s c and attach to bumble bee behind head. ✿

Butterfly

Materials Required—
AMERICAN THREAD COMPANY
"STAR" PEARL COTTON, ARTICLE 90, SIZE 5

2—50 yd. Balls Black.
4—50 yd. Balls Yellow.
Kapok or Cotton for Filling.
Steel Crochet Hook No. 7.

BODY: With Black, ch 2 and work 3 s c in 1st st of ch, ch 1, turn.
2nd Row—1 s c in each s c working 2 s c in 1st and last s c, ch 1, turn.
3rd Row—1 s c in each s c, ch 1, turn.
Repeat last 2 rows 6 times, then work 22 rows even.
38th Row—1 s c in each s c decreasing 1 st at each side, (decrease: insert in st, pull through, insert in next st, pull through, thread over and work off all loops at one time), ch 1, turn.
Repeat last row twice.
41st Row—Same as 2nd row.
42nd Row—Same as 3rd row, then repeat last 2 rows once.
Next 4 Rows—1 s c in each s c.
49th Row—Same as 38th row, then work 2 rows even.
Repeat last 3 rows twice.
58th Row—Decrease every other st, break thread.
Work another section in same manner. Sew sections together on one side, fill with cotton and sew other side.
RIGHT WING: With Yellow, ch 20 and work 19 s c on ch, ch 1, turn.
2nd Row—1 s c in each s c working 2 s c in 1st and last s c, ch 1, turn.
3rd Row—1 s c in each s c, ch 1, turn.
Repeat last 2 rows 10 times.
24th Row—2 s c in 1st s c, 1 s c in each of the next 22 s c, ch 1, turn.
25th Row—Decrease 1 sc at beginning of row, 1 s c in each remaining s c, ch 1, turn.
26th Row—2 s c in 1st s c, 1 s c in each remaining s c, ch 1, turn.
Repeat last 2 rows 5 times, then repeat 25th row once, ch 1, turn.
38th Row—Decrease 1 s c at beginning and end of row, ch 1, turn.
Next 4 Rows—Repeat 38th row, break thread.
Skip 1 st of 23rd row, join thread in next st and work 1 s c in each remaining s c increasing 1 s c in last s c, ch 1, turn.
Next Row—1 s c in each s c decreasing 1 s c at end of row, ch 1, turn.
Next Row—1 s c in each s c decreasing 1 s c at beginning of row and increasing 1 s c at end of row.
Repeat last 2 rows once.
Next Row—1 s c in each s c decreasing 1 s c at end of row.
Next Row—1 s c in each s c decreasing 1 s c at beginning and end of row, break thread.
Work left wing in same manner. Sew wings together at center. Join Black at lower edge of wing and work a row of s c all around wings increasing a sufficient number of times around shaped edges to keep work flat and decreasing at indented parts of wings sufficiently to keep work flat, break Black. Join Yellow and work 4 rows in same manner, break Yellow. Join Black and work 1 s c in each s c increasing in same manner, break thread. With Yellow, embroider eyes using satin st, then embroider top of body as illustrated using outline st. With Black, embroider top of wing section as illustrated.
Dots are made in satin st, remainder of design is worked in outline st using double strand of thread.
Work another pair of wings for back of pot holder in same manner.
Sew wing sections together then sew to undersection of body. With Yellow, cover bone ring with s c and attach to butterfly behind head. ✿

Crab

Materials Required—

AMERICAN THREAD COMPANY
"DE LUXE" MERCERIZED CROCHET
AND KNITTING COTTON, ARTICLE 346

1—300 yd. Ball White,

"STAR" PEARL COTTON, ARTICLE 90, SIZE 5

1—50 yd. Ball Red and

"STAR" SIX STRAND MERCERIZED
EMBROIDERY COTTON, ARTICLE 50

1 skein Black.

Steel Crochet Hook No. 7.

With White, ch 67, s c in 3rd st from hook, **1 s c** in next st of ch, * **ch 1,** skip 1 st of ch, **1 s c** in each of the next 2 sts, repeat from * across row, ch 2, turn.

2nd Row—Skip 1 s c, 2 s c in next s c, * ch 1, skip 1 s c, 2 s c in next s c, repeat from * across row, ch 2, turn. Work should measure about 6 inches. Repeat the 2nd row until work meas-

continued on next page

CRAB *(continued)*
ures 6 inches, break thread. Work another section in same manner.
CRAB: With Red, ch 2, 2 s c in 2nd st from hook, ch 1 to turn each row.
2nd Row—2 s c in each s c.
3rd Row—2 s c in 1st s c, 1 s c in each of the next 2 s c, 2 s c in last s c.
4th and 5th Rows—1 s c in each s c.
6th and 7th Rows—Increase 1 s c at beginning and end of each row.
8th Row—Work even. Repeat the last 3 rows twice.
15th Row—Increase 1 s c at beginning and end of row, then work 1 row even.
17th Row—Same as 15th row, then work 9 rows even.
27th Row—Decrease 1 s c at beginning and end of row, then work 1 row even.
Repeat the last 2 rows.
31st and 32nd Rows—Same as 27th row, then work 1 row even.
Next 2 Rows—Decrease 1 s c at beginning and end of each row, then work 2 rows even.
Next 3 Rows—Same as 27th row, then work 1 row even.
Next Row—* Skip 1 s c, insert needle in next s c, pull loop through, repeat from * once, thread over and pull through all loops on needle at one time, without breaking thread, ch 3, d c in same space, then work a row of s c around entire shell working 2 d c at opposite end, break thread.
CLAW: With Red, ch 4, s c in 2nd st from hook, 1 s c in each of the next 2 sts of ch, ch 1 to turn each row.
2nd Row—1 s c in each s c. Repeat the 2nd row 8 times.
11th Row—Skip 1 s c, 1 s c in each of the next 2 s c.
12th Row—1 s c in each s c. Repeat last row 5 times.
18th Row—Skip 1 s c, s c in next s c.
19th Row—1 s c in s c. Repeat last row twice, break thread. Work 7 more claws in same manner.
FRONT CLAW: With Red, ch 5 and work 4 s c on ch, ch 1 to turn each row.
2nd Row—1 s c in each s c.
3rd Row—Increase 1 s c at beginning and end of row, then work 8 rows even.
12th Row—Decrease 1 s c at beginning and end of row, then work 2 rows even.
15th Row—1 s c in next s c, s d c in next s c, (s d c: thread over needle, insert in st, pull through, thread over and work off all loops at one time) d c in next c, 2 tr c in last s c, ch 4, turn.
16th Row—2 tr c in same space with ch 4, 1 d c in each of the next 2 sts, 1 s c in each of the next 2 sts, ch 1, turn.
17th Row—1 s c in each st omitting the end ch.
18th and 19th Rows—1 s c in each s c.
20th Row—Increase 1 s c at end of row, then work 7 rows even.
28th Row—1 s c in each of the next 4 s c, ch 1, turn.
29th Row—Decrease 1 st, 1 s c in each of the next 3 s c, ch 1, turn.
30th Row—Decrease 1 st, 1 s c in each of the next 2 s c, ch 1, turn, 1 s c in each of the next 2 s c, ch 1, turn, skip 1 s c, 1 s c in last s c, ch 1, turn, 1 s c in s c, break thread. Attach thread in 1st free st at center of 27th row and work 1 s c in same space, 1 s c in each of the next 2 s c, ch 1, turn, * 1 s c in each s c, ch 1, turn, repeat from * once, skip 1 s c, 1 s c in each of the next 2 s c, ch 1, turn, 1 s c in each s c, ch 1, turn, skip 1 s c, s c in s c, ch 1, turn, s c in s c, break thread. Work another front claw in same manner.
Sew shell of crab to center of top section starting about 2½ inches from top. Sew the 2 front claws in position about 1½ inches from side point of shell. Sew other claws in position as illustrated bending claws as desired.
With Black Six Strand Embroidery Cotton, embroider eyes and feelers using a satin stitch for eyes. Indicate the joints of each claw and embroider body as illustrated.
With Red, crochet the two sections together as follows: * ch 2, d c in same space, skip the length of a d c, s c in next st, repeat from * all around. With Red, cover a bone hook and attach to top of potholder. ✿

Fish

Materials Required—
AMERICAN THREAD COMPANY
"DE LUXE" MERCERIZED CROCHET
AND KNITTING COTTON, ARTICLE 346
1—300 yd. Ball White and **"STAR" PEARL COTTON,** Article 90, Size 5.
2—50 yd. Balls Red.
"STAR" SIX STRAND MERCERIZED
EMBROIDERY COTTON, ARTICLE 50
1 yd. Black.
Steel Crochet Hook No. 7.
With White, ch 2, 3 s c in 1st st of ch, ch 1 to turn each row.
2nd Row—Working in s c and picking up back loop of st only throughout, increase 1 s c at beginning and end of row.
Repeat 2nd row 5 times.
8th Row—Increase 2 s c at beginning and end of row.
9th Row—Repeat 8th row.
Repeat 2nd row 8 times, then work 4 rows even, drop White.
22nd Row—Attach Red (When changing Color always complete last half of st with next Color) and repeat 2nd row. Work 1 row even, drop Red.
24th Row—Pick up White and repeat 2nd row. Work 1 row even, drop White.
26th Row—Pick up Red and repeat 2nd row. Work 1 row even, drop Red.
Repeat the last 4 rows 3 times.
40th and 41st Rows—With White, work even.
42nd and 43rd Rows—With Red, work even. Repeat the last 4 rows twice.
52nd Row—With White, decrease 1 s c at beginning and end of row (To decrease: insert needle in st, pull through, insert needle in next st, pull through, thread over and pull through all loops at one time). Work 1 row even.
54th Row—With Red, decrease 1 s c at beginning and end of row. Work 1 row even.
56th and 57th Rows—With White, work even.
58th and 59th Rows—With Red, work even.
Repeat 52nd, 53rd, 54th and 55th rows 3 times.
Repeat 56th, 57th, 58th and 59th rows.
Repeat the 52nd, 53rd, 54th and 55th rows.
80th and 81st Rows—With White, decrease 1 s c at beginning and end of each row.
82nd and 83rd Rows—With Red, decrease 1 s c at beginning and end of each row. Repeat last 4 rows.
88th and 89th Rows—With White, work even.
90th and 91st Rows—With Red, increase 1 s c at beginning and end of each row, break Red.
Next 5 Rows—With White, work even.
97th Row—Increase 1 s c at beginning and end of row. Work 3 rows even.
101st Row—1 s c in each of the next 13 s c, ch 1, turn.
102nd Row—Decrease 1 s c at beginning and increase 1 s c at end of row.
103rd Row—Decrease 1 s c at end of row.
104th Row—Decrease 1 s c at beginning of row.
Repeat 103rd and 104th rows 4 times, then repeat 103rd row, break thread. Attach thread in 1st free s c of 100th row and work another tail section in same manner reversing shapings.
With Black "STAR" Six Strand Mercerized Embroidery Cotton, embroider eye and mouth in outline st as illustrated.
Crochet the two sections together as follows: starting at lower edge of head, with White, work a row of s c around head, break White. Attach Red and working along top edge, * ch 3, 3 d c in same space, skip 3 rows, s c in next row, repeat from * across striped section to tail, break Red. Attach White and crochet the tail sections together in same manner as head. With Red, work a row of s c across lower striped section.
With Red, cover a bone ring with s c and attach to back of head section. ✿

Turtle

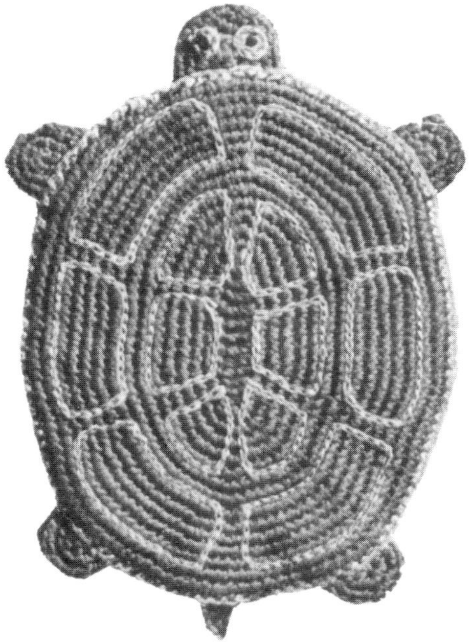

Shown in color on the inside front cover.

MATERIALS:

J. & P. COATS "KNIT-CRO-SHEEN," **Art. A.64:** 1 ball each of No. 48 Hunter's Green and No. 10-A Canary Yellow . . . **Milwards Steel Crochet Hook** No. 4 . . . A bone ring.

Use thread double throughout.

BODY . . . Starting at center with Hunter's Green, ch 14. **1st row:** Sc in 2nd ch from hook, half dc in next ch, dc in next 2 ch, tr in next 6 ch, dc in next 2 ch, sc in next ch. Now work in rnds. **1st rnd:** Working along opposite side of starting chain make 2 sc in first ch, sc in each ch across, 2 sc in last ch, sc in each st across. **2nd rnd:** Sc in each sc around, increasing 2 sc over each end and 2 sc on each long side—*to inc 1 sc, make 2 sc in 1 sc.* **3rd rnd:** Sc in each sc around, increasing 2 sc over both ends. Repeat 2nd and 3rd rnds alternately until 13 rnds have been completed. **14th and 15th rnds:** Sc in each sc around. Break off at end of 15th rnd. Attach a single strand of Canary Yellow and sc in each st around. Join and break off. With Canary Yellow, embroider markings on back in chain st.

STOMACH . . . Using Canary Yellow, work exactly as for Body until 15 rnds have been completed. Break off

HEAD . . . Starting at center with Green, ch 7. **1st rnd:** 3 sc in 2nd ch from hook, sc in each ch across, 3 sc in last ch; working along opposite side of starting chain, sc in each ch across. **2nd, 3rd and 4th rnds:** Sc in each sc around, increasing 3 sc evenly at each rounded end. Break off at end of 4th rnd.

LEG (Make 4) . . . Work as for Head until 3 rnds have been completed. Break off at end of 3rd rnd.

TAIL . . . With Hunter's Green, ch 4. **1st row:** 2 dc in 4th ch from hook. Ch 3, turn. **2nd row:** Dc in first 2 dc, dc in top of turning chain. Break off.

Fold Head in half and sew together around rounded end. Sew in place on Body. Complete Legs the same way. Sew Tail to Body.

For Padding, see page 2.

Sew Stomach piece in place.

EYE (Make 2) . . . With double strand of Yellow, ch 2. 7 sc in 2nd ch from hook. Join and break off.

Sew Eyes to Head with a piece of Black embroidery floss, making a French knot in center of each Eye.

With Yellow, sc closely around bone ring. Sew in place. ✿

Ladybug

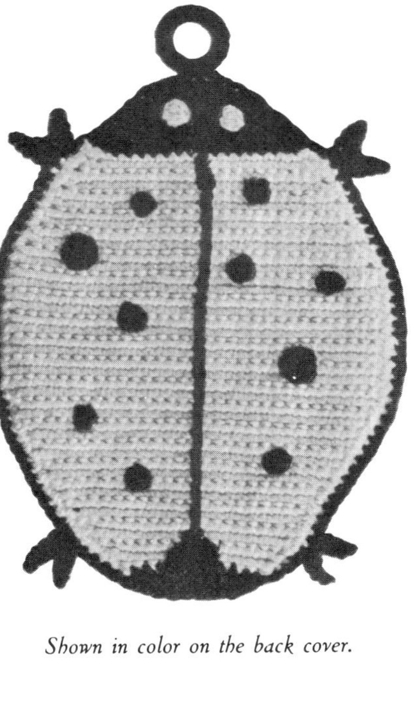

Shown in color on the back cover.

MATERIALS:

J. & P. COATS "KNIT-CRO-SHEEN," **Art. A.64:** 2 balls of No. 123-A Flamingo and 1 ball of No. 12 Black . . . **Milwards Steel Crochet Hook** No. 4 . . . A bone ring.

FRONT . . . Starting at top with a double strand of Black, ch 6. **1st row:** 2 sc in 2nd ch from hook, sc in each ch across, 2 sc in last ch. Ch 1, turn. **2nd to 8th rows incl:** 2 sc in first sc (1 sc increased), sc in each sc across, 2 sc in last sc. Ch 1, turn. At end of 8th row break off and turn. Attach double strand of Flamingo to first sc. **9th row:** Repeat 2nd row. Continue to work in pattern until there are 22 sts on row. Ch 1, turn. Inc 1 sc at beginning of every row until there are 32 sts on row. Now work without increasing until piece measures $4\frac{1}{2}$ inches in all. Dec 1 sc at beginning of every row until 18 sts remain—*to dec 1 sc, work off 2 sc as 1 sc.* Dec 1 sc at both ends for the next 3 rows. Break off and turn. Attach Black, dec 1 sc at both ends for the next 2 rows. Join and break off. Attach a double strand of Flamingo to first Flamingo row and, working across Flamingo only, sc in the end st of each row. Break off. Complete other side to correspond.

CENTER STRIPE . . . With Black make a chain $6\frac{1}{2}$ inches long. 4 dc in the 4th ch from hook. Break off. Sew in place.

EYE (Make 2) . . . Starting at center with a single strand of Flamingo, ch 2. **1st rnd:** 7 sc in 2nd ch from hook. Join and break off. Sew Eyes in place at top of pot holder.

SMALL DOT (Make 8) . . . Starting at center with Black, ch 2. Work as for first rnd of Eye.

LARGE DOT (Make 2) . . . Starting at center with Black, ch 3. **1st rnd:** 9 half dc in 3rd ch from hook. Join and break off. Sew Dots in place.

BACK . . . Work exactly as for Front.

For Padding, see page 2.

With wrong sides facing and working through both thicknesses, attach a double strand of Black and with a No. 4 hook, sc closely around Body. Join and break off.

LEG (Make 8) . . . Using a double strand of Black, ch 4. **1st row:** 2 dc in 4th ch from hook. Ch 4, turn. **2nd row:** Sl st in 2nd ch from hook, sc in next 2 ch, skip 1 dc, sl st in next dc, ch 4, sl st in 2nd ch from hook, sc in next 2 ch, sl st in top of turning chain. Break off. Sew 2 leg pieces together for each leg. Sew Legs in place.

With Black, sc closely around bone ring. Sew in place. ✿

Lobster

MATERIALS:

J. & P. Coats "Knit-Cro-Sheen," Art. A.64, 1 ball of No. 25 Crystal Blue; or

Clark's O.N.T. Mercerized Bedspread Cotton, Art. B.504, colors of your own choice; or

J. & P. Coats or Clark's O.N.T. Pearl Cotton, Art. A. or B.19, Size 5, 1 ball of No. 8 Blue; and

Clark's Big Ball Three Cord Mercerized Crochet, Art. B.34, Size 20, 1 ball of No. 123-A Flamingo.

Milwards Steel Crochet Hook No. 7.

A piece of blue felt for lining.

A bone ring.

Starting at lower edge with Crystal Blue make a chain 7 inches long. **1st row:** Sc in 2nd ch from hook and in each ch across until row measures 5½ inches. Cut off remaining chain. Ch 1, turn. **2nd row:** Sc in each sc across. Ch 1, turn. Repeat 2nd row until piece measures 5½ inches from starting chain. Break off.

BORDER . . . 1st rnd: Attach a double strand of Flamingo to any corner, 3 sc in same place, sc closely around outer edge making 3 sc in each corner. Join with sl st to first sc. **2nd and 3rd rnds:** Ch 1, sc in each sc around, making 3 sc in center sc of 3-sc group at each corner. Join. Break off at end of 3rd rnd.

LOBSTER—Body . . . With double strand of Flamingo, ch 16. **1st row:** Dc in 4th ch from hook and in each ch across, 5 dc in last ch. Working along opposite side of starting chain, dc in each ch across. Ch 3, turn. **2nd row:** Skip first dc, dc in each st around, making 2 dc in each of the 3 center dc of 5-dc group at rounded end. Ch 1, turn. **3rd row:** Sc in first dc, (ch 8, sl st in 3rd ch from hook, ch 3, sl st in 3rd ch from hook, sl st in next 5 ch—small claw—sc in next 2 dc) 4 times; sc in next 6 dc, ch 3, sl st in side of last sc made—eye—sc in next 2 dc, ch 27, sl st in 2nd ch from hook and in each ch across—feeler—sc in next 4 dc, ch 27, complete feeler and other side to correspond. Break off.

MEDIUM CLAW . . . Attach double strand of Flamingo to first sc following first set of small claws made, ch 30. **1st row:** Sl st in 2nd ch from hook, sc in next 12 ch, (skip next ch, sc in next 3 ch) 3 times; skip next ch, sc in each remaining chain, sl st in next 2 sc on Body. Turn. **2nd row:** Sc in each sc across to within last 11 sc, sl st in next sc, (in next sc make sl st, ch 3 and sl st, sl st in next 2 sc) twice; in next sc make sl st, ch 3 and sl st—teeth. Break off. **3rd row:** With wrong side of last row facing, attach double strand of Flamingo to 3rd sc following teeth, sc in next 3 sc, ch 15, sl st in 2nd ch from hook, sc in next ch, half dc in next ch, 2 dc in next ch, dc in next 2 ch, 2 dc in next ch, dc in next ch, half dc in each remaining ch, holding back on hook the last loop of each dc, make dc in side of next half dc, in base of same half dc and in next st, thread over and draw through all loops on hook (cluster made), (work off next 3 sc as 1 sc) twice; sc in each remaining st, sl st in Body. Break off.

LARGE CLAW . . . With wrong side of last row of Body facing, attach double strand of Flamingo to first sc following claws, ch 50. **1st row:** Sl st in 2nd ch from hook, sl st in next 2 ch, skip next ch, (sc in next 5 ch, work off next 2 sc as 1 sc) 4 times; sc in next 2 ch, work off next 2 sc as 1 sc, sc in next 12 ch, sl st in next 2 sts on Body. Turn. **2nd row:** (Sc in next 3 sc, work off 2 sc as 1 sc) twice; half dc in next sc, dc in next sc, work off next 2 dc as 1 dc, dc in next 3 sc, (work off 2 dc as 1 dc, dc in next sc) 6 times; work off 2 sc as 1 sc, sc in next 3 sc, sl st in next 3 sc. Turn. **3rd row:** (In next st make sl st, ch 3 and sl st, sl st in next st) twice; ch 3, sl st in 3rd ch from hook, sc in next 2 sts, (ch 3, sl st in 3rd ch from hook, half dc in next 2 sts) twice; dc in next 12 sts; ch 21, sl st in 2nd ch from hook, sc in next ch, half dc in next 3 ch, dc in next 3 ch, 2 dc in next ch, tr in next 5 ch, dc in next 6 ch, make a 5-dc cluster by making 2 dc in side of next dc, dc in base of same dc and dc in next 2 sts, half dc in next st, sc in each remaining st, sl st in Body. Break off.

TAIL . . . Starting at lower end, ch 11. **1st row:** Dc in 4th ch from hook, dc in each ch across, 2 dc in last ch. Ch 1, turn. **2nd row:** Sl st in back loop of each dc across. Ch 3, turn. **3rd row:** Working in back loop of previous dc row make 3 dc in first dc, dc in each dc across to within last 3 dc, 3 dc in next dc. Ch 1, turn. Repeat 2nd and 3rd rows alternately 3 more times. Break off.

Now work as follows: With wrong side of first dc row facing, attach double strand of Flamingo to first ch on opposite side of starting chain. **1st row:** Sl st in each ch across. Ch 4, turn. **2nd row:** 4 tr in back loop of first sl st, tr in back loop of each sl st across, 5 tr in back loop of last sl st. Ch 1, turn. **3rd row:** Skip first tr, sl st in next 2 tr, in next tr make sc, 2 half dc and sc; half dc in next tr, dc in next tr, 3 tr in next tr, dc in next tr, half dc in next tr, in next tr make sc, 2 half dc and sc. Break off.

Sew Lobster in place on pot holder. Attach double strand of Flamingo to bone ring. Sc closely around ring. Break off. Sew to corner. Cut felt to size and sew in place for lining.

Clown

MATERIALS:

J. & P. COATS "KNIT-CRO-SHEEN," **Art. A.64:** 1 ball each of No. 1 White, No. 49 Chartreuse Green and No. 126 Spanish Red . . . A few yards of No. 12 Black . . . **Milwards Steel Crochet Hook** No. 7 . . . A bone ring.

FRONT—Hat . . . Starting at top with Spanish Red, ch 2. **1st row:** 2 sc in 2nd ch from hook. Ch 1, turn. **2nd row:** 2 sc in first sc (1 sc increased), sc in next sc. Ch 1, turn. **3rd row:** 2 sc in first sc, sc in each sc across. Ch 1, turn. Repeat 3rd row until there are 38 sts on last row. Break off and turn.

HEAD . . . Attach White to beginning of row and continue to work in pattern until there are 46 sts on last row. Work 3 rows without increasing. Inc 1 st at beginning of next 2 rows. Repeat last 5 rows once more. Work without increasing until Head measures 3½ inches. Dec 1 sc at beginning of next 6 rows—*to dec 1 sc, work off 2 sc as 1 sc*—then dec 1 sc at both ends of next 8 rows. Work 3 more rows without decreasing. Break off.

EAR (Make 2) . . . With White, ch 16. **1st row:** 4 dc in 4th ch from hook, dc in each ch across, 5 dc in last ch. Ch 1, turn. **2nd row:** Sc in first dc, 2 sc in next 3 dc, sc in each dc across to within last 4 dc, 2 sc in next 3 dc, sc in top of starting chain. Ch 1, turn. **3rd row:** Sc in each sc across. Ch 1, turn. **4th row:** Sc in first sc, 2 sc in next 3 sc, sc in each sc across to within last 4 sc, 2 sc in next 3 sc, sc in next sc. Break off. Sew Ears in place. With a single strand of Black embroider outline.

NOSE . . . Starting at center with Spanish Red, ch 2. **1st rnd:** 6 sc in 2nd ch from hook. **2nd rnd:** 2 sc in each sc around. **3rd rnd:** * 2 sc in next sc, sc in next sc. Repeat from * around. Break off. Sew Nose in place.

HAT TRIMMING . . . Using a double strand of Chartreuse make a chain 5 inches long. Sc in 2nd ch from hook, draw loop on hook out to measure ½ inch, holding last loop on hook, insert hook in same ch and draw loop through, thread over and draw through 2 loops on hook, draw loop on hook out to same height as previous loop (another loop st made). Make 2 loop sts in each ch across, 5 loop sts in last ch; working along opposite side of starting chain, make 2 loop sts in each ch across, make 3 loop sts in last ch. Join and break off. Sew Trimming to Hat.

Make another piece, starting with ch 3, sc in 2nd ch from hook, make 4 loop sts in same place, 4 loop sts in next ch, working along opposite side of starting chain, make 4 loop sts in next 2 ch. Join and break off. Sew to top of Hat.

COLLAR . . . Work as for Hat Trimming making a chain 3¼ inches long. Join and break off. Sew in place.

With Black embroider eyes on Face. With Spanish Red embroider mouth.

BACK . . . Work exactly as for Front. For Padding, see page 2.

Sew pieces together. With Chartreuse sc closely around a bone ring and sew in place at top of Hat. ✿

Parasol

MATERIALS:

J. & P. COATS "KNIT-CRO-SHEEN," **Art. A.64:** 2 balls of No. 46-A Mid Rose and 1 ball of No. 12 Black . . . **Milwards Steel Crochet Hook** No. 7 . . . A bone ring.

Starting at pointed end with Mid Rose, ch 2. **1st row:** 2 sc in 2nd ch from hook. Ch 1, turn. **2nd row:** 3 sc in each sc. Ch 1, turn. **3rd row:** Sc in each sc across. Ch 1, turn. **4th row:** Sc in first sc, 3 sc in next sc, sc in next 2 sc, 3 sc in next sc, sc in next sc. Ch 1, turn. **5th row:** Sc in each sc across. Ch 1, turn. **6th row:** Sc in next 2 sc, 3 sc in next sc, sc in next sc, work off next 2 sc as 1 sc (1 sc decreased), sc in next sc, 3 sc in next sc, sc in next 2 sc. Ch 1, turn. **7th row:** Sc in each sc across. Ch 1, turn. **8th row:** Mark center sc over previous 3 sc groups, and previous decrease, sc in each sc across, making 3 sc over center sc of previous 3 sc groups and decreasing 1 sc over previous decrease. Ch 1, turn. Repeat 7th and 8th rows alternately until piece measures 6¾ inches from pointed end. Now work sc closely around pointed end to opposite side of last row. Join and break off.

RUFFLE . . . 1st row: Attach Black to last row and sc in each sc across. Ch 7, turn. **2nd row:** Sc in 3rd ch from hook (picot made), * ch 1, dc in next sc, ch 4, sc in 3rd ch from hook (another picot made). Repeat from * across, ending with dc in last sc. Break off. With Black embroider ch sts along each increased section.

TRIM . . . With Black make a chain

continued on next page

PARASOL *(continued)*

10 inches long. Sc in 3rd ch from hook, * skip 5 ch, dc in next ch, ch 1, picot, ch 1. Repeat from * across, ending with dc. Break off.

Make another piece 6½ inches long, and one piece 2½ inches long. Sew in place, spacing evenly apart.

Make other side of parasol the same way, omitting edging at bottom.

HANDLE . . . Cut 6 strands of Black each 12 inches long. With Black make a chain 10½ inches, do not break off but sc closely around bone ring, sl st in first sc; then, working over 6 strands of Black, make sc in each ch across, 5 sc in last ch, still working over 6 strands, and along opposite side of starting chain, make sc in next 10 ch, sl st in next ch. Break off. Trim strands neatly.

For Padding, see page 2.

Sew handle securely inside one piece, having doubled end at pointed end of parasol. Sew pieces together.

Honeymoon Cottage

Shown in color on the front cover.

MATERIALS REQUIRED:

Art. 600 Lily Cotton Yarn Skeins **or**
Art. 930 Sugar 'N Cream Yarn Balls
1 skein or ball; Red, Lt. Blue **and**
Art. 21 Lily Six Strand Floss
1 skein each; Lt. Yellow, Dk. Green and Scarlet. 2 skeins Dk. Brown.
Crochet Hooks Nos. 0 and 5.

FRONT—Roof—With Red Yarn and No. 0 hook, ch 40, 3 dc in 5th ch from hook, sk next 2 ch, sc in next ch, (ch 3, 3 dc in next ch, sk next 2 ch, sc in next ch) 8 times. **ROW 2**—Ch 3, turn, sc in ch-3 of 1st shell, (ch 3, 3 dc in same place, sc in ch-3 of next shell) repeated across (1 less shell than last row). Repeat Row 2 thru Row 9 (1 shell left.) Fasten off. **Wall**—With Lt. Blue ch 25, sk 3 ch, hdc in remaining 22 ch. **ROW 2**—Ch 2, turn, hdc in each hdc across (same number as last row). Do not work in end ch in this row. **ROW 3**—Ch 2, turn, hdc in each hdc across, hdc in end ch-2 (1 more hdc than last row). Repeat Row 3 once and Row 2 twice (thru Row 6). Fasten off. Sew Row 1 of Roof over top of Wall.

Window—With Yellow Floss and No. 5 hook, ch 10, sk 3 ch, dc in next 7 ch. **ROW 2**—Ch 3, turn, dc in 7 dc, dc in end ch-3. Fasten off. **ROW 3**—With Brown Floss, 2 sc in 1st dc in Row 2, * sc in next 6 dc, 3 sc in end st, 2 sc in 1st row down side, sc between rows, 2 sc in next row, * 3 sc in corner st. Repeat from * to *. Sc in 1st corner, join with sl st in 1st sc. Ch 4, sk 3 ch, sc in next ch, sc in same 1st sc, sc in each st across to center sc at next corner, ch 4 sk 3 ch, sc in next ch, sl st in same corner sc. Fasten off. Make two. Sew one on each side of Wall.

Door—With Brown, ch 17, sk 4 ch, dc in next 12 ch, 9 dc in end ch, dc in next 12 sts on other side of ch. **ROW 2**—Ch 2, turn, hdc in each dc with 2 dc in each of 7 dc around curved end. Fasten off. Sew on center of Wall. Make a Scarlet French Knot for door knob.

Lawn—With Green ch 45, sk 3 ch, dc in next 42 ch. **ROW 2**—Ch 3, turn, dc in back lps of 42 dc. Fasten off. Sew top of Row 2 over bottom edge of Wall.

Steps—With Scarlet ch 20, sk 3 ch, dc in next 17 ch. **ROW 2**—Ch 3, turn, dc in back lps of 17 dc. Fasten off. **ROW 3**—Join to 3d dc in last row, ch 3, dc in back lps of next 12 dc. Fasten off. Sew top of Row 3 across base of Door. On Wall above Lawn (each side of Door), embroider Lazy Daisy Stitch Leaves in Green, then scatter French Knots in Scarlet among the Leaves.

Chimney—With Brown ch 2, 2 sc in 2d ch from hook. **ROW 2**—Ch 2, turn, hdc in 1st sc, 2 hdc and dc in next sc. **ROW 3**—Ch 3, turn, dc and 2 hdc in 1st st, hdc in each hdc across. **ROW 4**—Ch 2, turn, hdc in each hdc across with 2 hdc and dc in end dc. **ROWS 5 thru 7**—(Ch 2, turn, hdc in 8 hdc) 3 times. **ROW 8**—Ch 4, turn, sk 3 ch, hdc in next ch, hdc in next 8 hdc, ch 4, sk 3 ch, hdc in next ch, sl st in same st with previous hdc. Fasten off. Make 2 pieces and sew tog. back-to-back.

BACK—Repeat Roof and Wall. Sew to Front, inserting Chimney between 2 Roof pieces on left side. Turn Row 1 of Lawn up and sew to bottom edge of Back. Turn Row 1 of Steps up at back and hem down. Cover a bone ring with sc in Red and sew on Back 1" below top of Roof. Steam and press Holder dry on back thru a cloth.

Shown in color on the front cover.

Easter Bonnet

MATERIALS REQUIRED:
Art. 600—Lily Cotton Yarn Skeins **or**
Art. 930 Sugar 'N Cream Yarn Balls:
1 skein or ball Yellow **and**
Art. 39 Lily Pearl Cotton Size 5
1 ball each; White and Pink.
Art. 21 Lily Six Strand Floss
1 skein Shaded Greens and scraps of Lavender, Dk. Rose, Med. Blue and Dk. Yellow.
Crochet Hooks Nos. 0 and 5.

FRONT—Crown—With Yellow Yarn and No. 0 hook, ch 19, sk 1 ch, sc in next 18 ch. **ROW 2**—Ch 3, turn, 2 dc in 1st sc, * dc in next 4 sc, holding back the last lp of each dc on hook, make dc in next 2 sc, yarn over and draw thru all lps on hook (a Cluster-decrease made). Repeat from * once, dc in next 5 sc. **ROW 3**—Ch 3, turn, dc in 17 dc. **ROW 4**—Ch 1, turn, sc in 1st 2 dc, hdc in next dc, dc in next 3 dc, 2 dc in next dc, dc in next 10 dc. **ROW 5**—Ch 1, turn, sk 1 dc and working in back lps only, make sc in next st, hdc in next 2 sts, dc in next 2 sts, 2 dc in next st, dc in next 3 sts, hdc in next 3 sts, sc in next 3 sts, sl st in next 2 sts. Fasten off.

Brim— With same side up, join to 1st st on opposite side of starting ch, ch 1, 3 sc in same st, hdc in next 2 sts, (dc in next 4 sts, 2 dc in next st) 3 times. **ROW 2**—Ch 3, turn, (dc in 5 dc, 2 dc in next dc) 3 times, dc in next 2 sts, hdc in next 2 sts, sc in next st. **ROW 3**—Ch 1, turn, sc in 1st 2 sts, hdc in next 2 sts, dc in next 2 sts, 2 dc in next st, dc in next 20 sts. **ROW 4**—Ch 3, turn, (dc in 5 sts, 2 dc in next st) twice, dc in next 2 sts, hdc in next 3 sts, 2 hdc in next st, sc in next 10 sts. **ROW 5**—Ch 1, turn, (sc in next 4 sts, 2 sc in next st) twice, (hdc in next 4 sts, 2 hdc in next st) 3 times, hdc in next 7 sts. **ROW 6**—Ch 3, turn, (dc in 5 sts, 2 dc in next st) 5 times, dc in next 4 sts, hdc in next 2 sts, sc in next st. **ROW 7**—Ch 3, turn and working in back lps, (dc in 5 sts, 2 dc in next st) 7 times, dc in end st. Fasten off. **Lace Frill**—With White Pearl Cotton and No. 5 hook, join to front lp of 1st st in Row 6, ch 5, sc in same st, (ch 5, sc in front lp of next st) repeated across. **ROW 2**—Ch 7, turn, sc in 1st lp, (ch 5, sc in next lp) repeated across. **ROW 3**—Ch 1, turn, sc thru both last sc and the dc directly behind in Row 7, * ch 3, sc in next lp, ch 2, a 2 dc, ch 3, 2 dc shell in next lp, ch 2, sc in next lp, ch 3, sc thru next lp and top of dc directly behind lp. Repeat from * 10 times. Fasten off.

Ribbon—With Pink Pearl Cotton ch 30, dc in 4th ch from hook, tr in each ch across with dc in end ch. Fasten off. Sew one end between 3d and 4th Lace scallops from bottom corner, other end at base of Crown 1" from back edge.

Bow—With Pink, ch 85, 10 tr in 6th ch from hook, ** tr in next 9 ch, * dc in next 2 ch, hdc in next ch, sc in next ch, hdc in next ch, dc in next 2 ch, * (tr in next 20 ch, repeat from * to *) twice, tr in next 8 ch, 10 tr in end ch. Repeat from ** on other side of ch join to top of ch-5. Fasten off. Tack into a bow. **Bar**—Ch 12, sk 3 ch, dc in next 9 ch. Fasten off. Sew around center of Bow. Sew Bow at outside end of Ribbon.

No. 1—Flower—With Dk. Rose Floss, ch 7, join with sl st to form ring. **ROW 1**—Ch 1, 12 sc in ring, join to 1st sc. **ROW 2**—* Ch 3, 2 tr in next sc, ch 3, sl st in 3d ch from hook for a p, 2 tr in same sc on ring, ch 3, sc in next sc. Repeat from * 5 times. Fasten off. Make a Dk. Yellow French Knot at base of each petal. Make a 2d Flower in Lavender with Yellow Knots, and a 3d in Pink with Dk. Rose Knots.

No. 2 Flower—With Blue Floss, ch 4, draw out lp on hook to ¾" length, insert hook thru single back strand of long lp, thread over and draw thru, thread over and draw thru the 2 lps on hook, completing sc (Knot St Lp made). Sk 1 ch, sc in next ch, (a Knot St, sc in same ch) twice, sl st in next ch (center st of flower), * ch 2, a Knot St, sk 1 ch, sc in next ch, (Knot St, sc in same ch) twice, sl st in center st. Repeat from * twice. Fasten off. Make a Yellow French Knot in center. Make 2 Flowers.

Leaf—With Shd. Greens Floss * ch 9, ** 2 tr in 4th st from hook, ch 3, sl st in 3d ch from hook for a p, 2 tr in same ch with last tr, ch 3, sl st in same ch, sl st in next ch. ** Repeat from * once. Sl st in next 4 ch, ch 5, repeat from ** to **, sl st in 4 ch of stem. Fasten off. Make 4. Sew Flowers and Leaves around base of Crown as illustrated.

BACK—Repeat Crown and Brim except make Row 5 of Crown and Row 7 of Brim thru both lps of sts. Sew Back and Front tog. Cover a bone ring with Yellow sc. Sew to top of Bonnet. Steam and press Bonnet dry on back thru a cloth. ✿

Easter Egg

MATERIALS:

J. & P. COATS "KNIT-CRO-SHEEN," **Art. A.64:** 2 balls of No. 10-A Canary Yellow . . . **Milwards Steel Crochet Hook** No. 7 . . . A bone ring.

Starting at center of one end, ch 10. Join with sl st to form ring. **1st rnd:** Ch 5, d tr in ring, (ch 2, holding back on hook the last loop of each d tr, make 2 d tr in ring, thread over and draw through all loops on hook—cluster made) 11 times; ch 2, sl st in first d tr. **2nd rnd:** 3 sc in same place as sl st, (3 sc in next sp, sc in next cluster) 5 times; 3 sc in next sp, 3 sc in next cluster, (3 sc in next sp, sc in next cluster) 5 times; 3 sc in next sp. **3rd to 8th rnds incl:** Sc in back loop of each sc, making 3 sc in center sc of each 3 sc group. **9th rnd:** Ch 5, holding back on hook the last loop of each d tr, make 2 d tr in same place as last sc, and 3 d tr in center sc of next 3 sc group, thread over and draw through all loops on hook (joint d tr cluster made); * ch 10, make another joint cluster by making a 3 d tr cluster in same place as last cluster, skip 5 sc, cluster in next sc. Repeat from * around, ending with cluster in same place as first cluster, ch 10, sl st in tip of first cluster. **10th rnd:** Sc in same place as sl st, 10 sc in each sp and sc in tip of each joint cluster around. **11th and 12th rnds:** Sc in back loop of each sc around, making 3 sc in center sc at each end. **13th to 22nd rnds incl:** Sc in back loop of each sc around. **23rd rnd:** Ch 4, make a 2 tr cluster in same place as last sc, ch 4, 2 tr in tip of last cluster, ch 4, sc in same place as first cluster and in next 10 sc, * ch 9, 2 tr cluster in 5th ch from hook, 3 tr cluster in same place as last sc, ch 4, 2 tr cluster in tip of last cluster, ch 4, sc in same sc as last cluster was made and in next 10 sc. Repeat from * around, ending with ch 9, 2 tr cluster in 5th ch from hook. Join to top of starting ch-4. **24th rnd:** Ch 4, 2 tr cluster in same place, * ch 5, sc between next 2 clusters, ch 5, cluster between next 2 clusters. Repeat from * around, ending with sl st in tip of first cluster. **25th rnd:** Sc in same place as sl st, * ch 10, sc in tip of next cluster. Repeat from * around. Join. **26th rnd:** Sc in each sc and each ch around. **27th to 30th rnds incl:** Sc in back loop of each sc around. **31st rnd:** * Sc in back loop of next 3 sc, ch 3. Repeat from * around. Join and break off. Make another piece the same way.

For Padding see page 2. (Use a colored piece of felt or colored outing flannel). Slip end of pot holder over padding and sew ch 3 loops together at center.

Sc closely around bone ring and sew in place. ✿

Palette

MATERIALS:

J. & P. COATS "KNIT-CRO-SHEEN," **Art. A.64:** 3 balls of No. 64 Platinum, 1 ball of No. 126 Spanish Red . . . A few yards of No. 12 Black and 5 more assorted colors . . . **Milwards Steel Crochet Hooks** No. 4 and No. 7 . . . A bone ring.

Use Platinum double throughout.

PALETTE . . . Starting at bottom with Platinum and No. 4 hook, ch 11. **1st row:** Sc in 2nd ch from hook and each ch across. Ch 1, turn. **2nd row:** 2 sc in first sc (1 sc increased), sc in each sc across, 2 sc in last sc. Ch 1, turn. Repeat 2nd row until there are 30 sc on row. Then inc 1 sc at beginning of each row until there are 45 sc on row. Work without increasing until piece measures 5 inches long. Dec 1 sc —*to dec 1 sc, work off 2 sc as 1 sc*— at beginning of every other row until there are 35 sc on row.

To Shape Top: 1st row: Dec 1 sc, sc in next 16 sc. Ch 1, turn. **2nd row:** Dec 1 sc, sc in each sc across. Ch 1, turn. Repeat 2nd row until 8 sc remain. Break off. Attach thread to next free sc on last complete row, dec 1 sc, sc in each sc across to within last 2 sc, dec 1 sc. Ch 1, turn. Repeat last row until 5 sc remain. Break off. Attach a double strand of Spanish Red and sc closely around. Join and break off.

COLOR DABS . . . With single strand of Black and No. 7 hook, ch 2. **1st rnd:** 7 sc in 2nd ch from hook. **2nd rnd:** 2 sc in each sc around. Inc 7 sc evenly on each rnd until piece measures $1\frac{1}{4}$ inches in diameter. Join and break off.

Make 1 Red and 5 more in assorted colors. Sew in place.

BRUSH (Make 2) . . . Starting at long side with Black and No. 7 hook, ch 20. **1st row:** Sc in 2nd ch from hook and in next 3 ch, half dc in next 6 ch, dc in next 9 ch. Break off. Sew sc end to Black color dab. With Black embroider bristles on brushes.

Make another piece the same way.

For Padding, see page 2.

Working through both thicknesses and using a single strand of Red, sl st in back loop of each sc around. Join and break off. With Red sc closely around bone ring. Sew in place. ✿

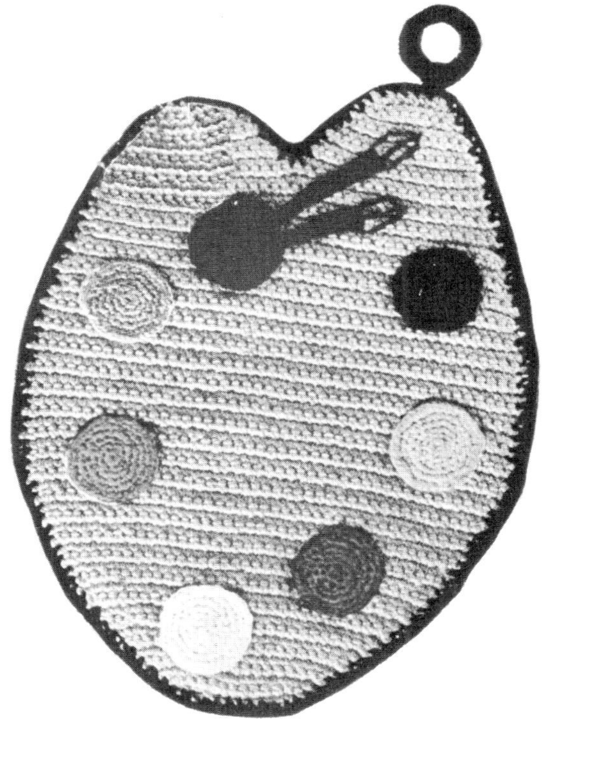

Gingerbread Boy

This holder may be made with any of the American Thread Company products listed below:

Material	Quantity	Size of Needle
"DE LUXE" Crochet Cotton		
Article 346	2 Balls White	Steel 3
or		
"PURITAN" Crochet Cotton		
Article 40	2 Balls White	Steel 3
and		
"STAR" Pearl Cotton		
Article 90, Size 5	1 Ball Brown	Steel 7

Entire potholder is made with double strand of cotton.
FRONT SECTION: Starting at lower edge of leg with White and No. 3 hook, ch 20, 2 s c in 2nd st from hook, 1 s c in each of the next 18 sts of ch, ch 1 to turn each row.
2nd Row. 1 s c in each s c (20 s c).
3rd Row. Skip 1 s c, 1 s c in each of the next 19 s c.
4th Row. 1 s c in each of the next 16 s c, decrease in next 2 sts (to decrease: * insert hook in next st, pull loop through, repeat from *, thread over and pull through all loops at one time).
5th Row. 1 s c in each s c increasing 1 s c at end of row (18 s c).
6th Row. Work even.
7th Row. Decrease in 1st 2 sts, 1 s c in each remaining s c.
8th Row. Work even.
9th Row. Same as 5th row.
10th Row. 1 s c in each s c decreasing 1 s c at end of row.
11th Row. Work even.
12th Row. Increase 1 s c at beginning of row, 1 s c in each remaining s c, break thread. Work another leg section in same manner but do not break thread, ch 1, turn.
13th Row. 1 s c in each s c, ch 1, pick up 1st section and with toe pointing to the left work 1 s c in each s c across 1st section, ch 1, turn.
14th Row. 1 s c in each s c working 1 s c on ch.
15th Row. Decrease 1 s c at beginning and end of row and work 3 rows even. Repeat the last 4 rows once.
23rd Row. Decrease 1 s c at beginning and end of row, then work 7 rows even, * ch 6 for arm, turn.
31st Row. 1 s c in 2nd st from hook, 1 s c in each remaining st of ch, 1 s c in each s c across row, ch 6 for other arm, turn.
32nd Row. 1 s c in 2nd st from hook, 1 s c in each remaining st of ch, 1 s c in each s c across row. Repeat from * once.
35th Row. Increase 1 s c at beginning and end of row, then work 1 row even.
37th Row. Decrease 1 s c at beginning and end of row, then work 1 row even.
39th Row. Skip 1 s c, 1 sl st in each of the next 5 s c, 1 s c in each remaining s c.
40th Row. Skip 1 s c, 1 sl st in each of the next 5 s c, 1 s c in each of the next 38 s c, ch 1, turn.
41st Row. 1 s c in each of the next 38 sts, ch 1, turn.
42nd Row. Skip 1 s c, 1 s c in each of the next 30 sts.
43rd Row. Skip 1 s c, 1 s c in each of the next 23 sts.
44th Row. Skip 1 s c, 1 s c in each of the next 20 sts.
45th Row. Skip 1 s c, 1 s c in each of the next 17 sts.
46th Row. Increase 1 s c at beginning and end of row, then work 1 row even.
48th Row. Increase 1 s c at beginning and end of row, then work 5 rows even.
54th and 55th Rows. Decrease 1 s c at beginning and end of each row, then work 1 row even.
57th, 58th and 59th Rows. Decrease 1 s c at beginning and end of each row.
60th Row. Skip 1 s c, sl st in next s c, 1 s c in each of the next 2 s c, 1 s d c in each of the next 4 s c (s d c: thread over hook, insert in st, pull through, thread over and pull through all loops at one time), 1 s c in each of the next 2 sts, sl st in next st, break thread.
UNDER SECTION: Work 1st 18 rows same as top section.
19th Row. Decrease 1 s c, 1 s c in each of the next 19 s c, ch 10 for thumb, skip 10 s c, 1 s c in each of the next 3 s c, decrease in next 2 s c, ch 1, turn.
20th Row. 1 s c in each s c and 1 s c in each st of ch. Work 2 rows even. Repeat from 23rd row of top section.
THUMB: Work 20 s c around thumb opening, then without joining rows work 11 more rows even.
Next Row. Decrease 5 sts evenly spaced, then work 3 rows even.
Decrease every other st until 8 sts remain, break thread leaving an end. Thread into needle and draw together, fasten firmly.
EDGE: Working on front section using a single strand of Brown "STAR" Pearl Cotton and No. 7 hook, * ch 3, d c in same space, skip about 1/8 inch space, sl st in next space, repeat from * around entire section.
EYES AND BUTTONS: With Brown "STAR" Pearl Cotton and No. 7 hook ch 2, 8 s c in 2nd st from hook, join, break thread leaving an end to sew. Work 4 more circles in same manner.
MOUTH: Work 1st row same as eyes.
2nd Row. 2 s c in each s c, join, break thread, leaving an end.
NOSE: With Brown, ch 5, join, break thread leaving an end to sew.
With Brown, ch 33, sl st in 3rd st from hook, * ch 3, skip 2 sts of ch, sl st in next st of ch, repeat from * across ch, break thread leaving an end. Sew in position to form lower edge of head. Sew Eyes, Nose, Mouth and Buttons in position as illustrated.
TRIM FOR FRONT: With Brown ch 36, sl st in 3rd st from hook, * ch 3, skip 2 sts of ch, sl st in next st, repeat from * across ch, break thread and work another strip in same manner. Sew on each side of buttons. Work 2 strips in same manner starting with ch 12 and sew on each arm as illustrated. Work 2 more strips in same manner starting with ch 27 and sew on each leg about 1/2 inch from lower edge.
Work edge around under section same as front section. Sew the 2 sections together leaving lower edge open for hand.
With White cover a bone ring with s c and sew to underside of holder.

The Sunbonnet Twins

POT HOLDERS or HOT PLATE MATS

MATERIALS REQUIRED:

Lily Sugar 'N Cream Yarn Art. 930

or

Lily Cotton Yarn Art. 600
1 ball or skein each in White, Cream and a color.

Steel Crochet Hook No. 1.

SIZE—Approximately 6 inches high; 6 inches wide.

FACE—With Ivory, ch 5, sk 1, sc in next 3 sts, 5 sc in next, sc in 3 on other side of ch, 5 sc in skipped st. Sc in next 4, 2 sc in next 3 sc, sc in 5, 2 sc in 3. (Sc in 6, [2 sc in next, sc in next] twice, 2 sc in next) twice. (Sc in 7, [2 sc in next, sc in next 2] twice, 2 sc in next) twice. (Sc in 8, [2 sc in 1, sc in 3] twice, 2 sc in next) twice. Sc in 11, 2 in 1, 1 in 4, 2 in 1, 1 in 14, 2 in 1, 1 in 4, 2 in 1, sc in next 48 sts, sl st in next 2 (44 sts around). Fasten off.

BONNET—Make 2 in White, 1 in color—sl st in last sc of face, working in back loop of sts around, sc in next 3 sts, hdc in 1, 2 dc in 1, dc in 1, 2 dc in 1, tr in 1, (2 tr in 1) 11 times, tr in 1, 2 dc in 1, dc in 1, 2 dc in 1, dc in 1, hdc in 1, sc in 3, sl st in 1. Fasten off. **ROW 2**—Sl st in first sc at beg of last row, ch 2, dc in back loop of next 7 sts, 2 dc in 1, dc in 2, 2 dc in 1, (tr in 2, 2 tr in 1) twice, (dtr—over hook 3 times—in 1, 2 dtr in 1) 4 times, (1 tr in 2, 2 in 1) twice, 2 dc in 1, dc in 2, 2 in 1, dc in 6. dc in next 2 holding final loop of each on hook, draw thread through all loops on hook at once. Fasten off. **ROW 3**—Sl st in first dc of last row, sc in back loop of each dc around, sl st in last st (51 sc, 2 sl st) around. Fasten off.

EDGE—(To contrast with Bonnet) Sl st in same st with first sl st in Row 1 of Bonnet, ch 3, sc in first st of ch for a picot (P), sl st in next 3-ch, (P, sl st) in next sl st and in back loop of each next second sc around, ending with sl st in same st with last sl st in Row 1. Fasten off.

AROUND FACE—With same color, ch 2, sl st, inserting needle in same sts used to work first row of bonnet, ch 2, fasten off. Tack ends at back. Fasten off.

BOW—With color (ch 8, sk 3, sc in 5) 3 times, sc in top at second tie, sc between first and second and 1 sc in top of first tie. Make a fourth tie same as first, sl st to first tie. Fasten off. Sew in place under chin.

HANGERS—Ch 16 and fasten off, leaving ends to sew in place.

Embroider the hair and features in color. Use yarn as it is for mouth and hair; split and use 2 ply for eyes, brows, nose. Make long stitches for eyebrows; tack in place with thread or yarn for smoother curves. You can design other faces from cartoon characters for variety. ✿

Shown in color on the inside front cover.

Snowman

MATERIALS:

J. & P. COATS "KNIT-CRO-SHEEN," Art. A.64: 2 balls of No. 1 White and 1 ball of No. 12 Black . . . A few yards of No. 123-A Flamingo . . . **Milwards Steel Crochet Hooks** No. 4 and No. 7 . . . A bone ring . . . 4 snap fasteners.

Use thread double throughout.

BODY—Front . . . Starting at center with White and No. 4 hook, ch 2. **1st rnd:** 7 sc in 2nd ch from hook. **2nd rnd:** 2 sc in each sc around. **3rd rnd:** * 2 sc in next sc (1 sc increased), sc in next sc. Repeat from * around. **4th rnd:** * 2 sc in next sc, sc in next 2 sc. Repeat from * around. Inc 7 sc evenly on each rnd until piece measures 6 inches in diameter. Join and break off.

HEAD . . . Work as for Body until piece measures 4 inches in diameter. Join and break off.

HAT . . . Starting at bottom with Black and No. 4 hook, ch 23. **1st row:** Sc in 2nd ch from hook and each ch across. Break off. **2nd row:** Skip first 5 sc. Attach thread to next sc, sc in same place and in next 11 sc. Ch 1, turn. **3rd row:** Inc 1 sc, sc in each sc across. Ch 1, turn. **4th row:** Sc in each sc across. Ch 1, turn. **5th row:** Repeat 3rd row. **6th to 12th rows incl:** Sc in each sc across. Ch 1, turn. Break off at end of 12th row. Sew Hat to Head.

EYE (Make 2) . . . Using Black and No. 4 hook, work as for Body until 2 rnds have been completed. Join and break off. Sew to Head.

NOSE . . . Using a single strand of Flamingo and No. 7 hook, ch 12. **1st row:** Sc in 2nd ch from hook and in each ch across. Ch 1, turn. **2nd row:** Dec 1 sc, sc in each sc across—*to dec 1 sc, work off 2 sc as 1 sc.* Ch 1, turn. Repeat 2nd row until 3 sc remain. Ch 1, turn. **Last row:** Work off 3 sc as 1 sc. Break off. Sew to Head.

MOUTH . . . Using a single strand of Black and No. 7 hook, ch 2. **1st rnd:** 7 sc in 2nd ch from hook. Join and break off. Make 3 more pieces the same way. Sew in place to form mouth.

BOW TIE . . . Using a double strand of Flamingo and No. 4 hook, ch 13. Work as for Nose until 5 sc remain. Dec 1 sc at both ends of next row. Work 2 rows without decreasing. Inc 1 st at both ends of next row, then inc 1 st at beginning of each row until there are 12 sc on last row. Break off. Sew to base of Head.

BUTTON (Make 3) . . . Work exactly as for Eyes. Sew in place on Body.

ARM (Make 2) . . . Using a single strand of Black and No. 7 hook, ch 25. Sl st in 2nd ch from hook and in next 5 ch, ch 8, sl st in 2nd ch from hook and in next 6 ch, sl st in same ch as last sl st was made on first limb, ch 6, sl st in 2nd ch from hook and in next 4 ch, sl st in same ch as last sl st was made on last limb, sl st in each remaining ch. Break off. Sew to Body.

BACK . . . Make another Body, Head and Hat.

For Padding, see page 2.

Sew Front and Back pieces together. Sew snap fasteners to Head and Body to join. With Black sc closely around bone ring. Sew to top of Hat. ✿

Christmas Tree

MATERIALS:

J. & P. COATS "KNIT-CRO-SHEEN," Art. A.64: 2 balls of No. 48 Hunter's Green, 1 ball of No. 126 Spanish Red . . . A few yards of No. 43 Dk. Yellow . . . **Milwards Steel Crochet Hook** No. 4 . . . A bone ring.

Use thread double throughout.

Starting at top with Hunter's Green, ch 2. **1st row:** 3 sc in 2nd ch from hook. Ch 1, turn. **2nd row:** 2 sc in first sc (1 sc increased), sc in next sc, 2 sc in next sc. Ch 1, turn. **3rd to 14th rows incl:** 2 sc in first sc, sc in each sc across, 2 sc in last sc. Ch 1, turn. **15th and 16th rows:** 2 sc in first sc, sc in each sc across to within last 4 sc. Ch 1, turn. Inc 1 sc at both ends of every row for 12 more rows. Repeat 15th and 16th rows, then continue increasing 1 sc at both ends of every row until piece measures 6 inches from top. Break off.

STAND . . . Starting at bottom with Spanish Red, ch 14. **1st row:** Sc in 2nd ch from hook and each ch across. Ch 1, turn. **2nd to 6th rows incl:** Sc in each sc across. Ch 1, turn. Break off at end of 6th row. Sew Stand to Tree.

TRIMMING . . . With Dk. Yellow make a chain 2 yards long. Sew in place on Tree.

ORNAMENT (Make 6) . . . With single strand of Red, ch 2. **1st rnd:** 6 sc in 2nd ch from hook. **2nd rnd:** 2 sc in each sc around. Join and break off. Sew in place on Tree.

Make another piece the same way.

For Padding, see page 2.

Sew pieces together. With single strand of Yellow, sc closely around bone ring. Sew in place. ✿

Christmas Ornament

Materials Required: AMERICAN THREAD COMPANY
The Famous "PURITAN" CROCHET COTTON, Article 40
1 ball each Red and White or colors desired and

"STAR" SIX STRAND EMBROIDERY COTTON, Article 50
1 skein Red or Lt. Emerald will make two pot holders.
Steel crochet hook No. 7 or No. 8.

Starting at top with Red ch 29, 2 d c in 4th st from hook, 1 d c in each of the next 24 sts of ch, 3 d c in last st, ch 3, turn. The ch 3 counts as 1 d c at beginning of each row.

2nd Row. 2 d c in same space (an increase of 2 d c), 1 d c in each of the next 28 d c, 3 d c in 3rd st of ch (an increase of 2 d c), ch 3 to turn all rows.

Next 3 Rows. Working in d c, increase 2 d c at beginning and end of each row (46 d c in last row).

6th Row. Increase 1 d c at beginning and end of row.

7th Row. Increase 2 d c at beginning and end of row, cut Red.

8th Row. Attach White, ch 3, 2 d c in same space, 1 d c in each d c, working 3 d c in 3rd st of end ch.

9th and 10th Rows. Increase 1 d c at beginning and end of each row. Work 2 rows even.

13th Row. Increase 1 d c at beginning and end of row. Work 5 rows even.

19th and 20th Rows. Decrease 1 d c at beginning and end of each row (to decrease: * thread over hook, insert in next d c, pull loop through and work off 2 loops, repeat from * once, thread over and work off all loops at one time). Work 1 row even.

22nd Row. Same as 19th row, cut White.

23rd Row. Attach Red, ch 3, decrease in next 2 sts, decrease in next 2 sts, 1 d c in each of the next 47 d c, decrease in next 2 sts, decrease in next 2 sts.

Next 4 Rows. Decrease 2 d c at beginning and end of each row.

Next Row. Decrease 3 sts each side, decreasing in same manner as previous rows, ch 1, turn.

Next Row. Insert hook in 1st st, pull loop through, insert in next st, pull loop through, thread over and work off all loops at one time, 1 s c in each of the next 2 sts, 1 s d c in each of the next 3 sts (s d c: thread over hook, insert in st, pull loop through, thread over and work off all loops at one time), 1 d c in each of the next 16 d c, 1 s d c in each of the next 3 d c, 1 s c in each of the next 2 sts, s c decrease in next 2 sts, ch 1, turn.

Next Row. S c decrease in 1st 2 sts, 1 s c in each of the next 3 sts, 1 s d c in each of the next 5 sts, 1 d c in each of the next 8 sts, 1 s d c in each of the next 5 sts, 1 s c in each of the next 3 sts, s c decrease in next 2 sts, cut thread. Work another section in same manner.

With Red or Lt. Emerald "STAR" SIX STRAND EMBROIDERY COTTON crochet a ch about 20 inches long. Sew in center of White section sewing to the 5 center rows as illustrated. Crochet the 2 sections together with a row of s c using Red on Red sections and White on White sections. With Lt. Emerald or Red cover a bone ring with s c and sew to top of pot holder. ✿

PANSY *(continued from page 16)*

2nd Row. 2 d c in same space, 3 d c in each remaining st.
3rd and 4th Rows. Same as 3rd row of Yellow petal.
5th Row. 1 d c in each st, ch 1, turn.
6th Row. 1 s c in each of the next 2 sts, 1 s d c in each of the next 2 sts, 1 d c in each of the next 15 sts, 1 s d c in each of the next 2 sts, 1 s c in each of the next 2 sts, ch 1, turn. Repeat last row twice, break Brown. Attach Brown in ring and work 1 more petal in same manner, break Brown.
Work a row of s c around entire petal working Yellow on Brown petals and Brown on the 3 Yellow petals.
With Green embroider the Yellow petals as illustrated using long and short stitches. Tack petals in position having the 2 Brown petals at top.
UNDER SECTION: With Yellow ch 2, 8 s c in 2nd st from hook, join in 1st s c.
2nd Row. Ch 1 and work 2 s c in each s c, do not join. Place a marker at beginning of each row.
3rd Row. Working in s c increase in every other s c.
4th Row. Increase in every 3rd s c.
5th Row. 1 s c in each of the next 2 s c, ch 8 for thumb opening, skip 6 s c, 1 s c in each remaining s c.
6th Row. * 1 s c in next st, 2 s c in next st, repeat from * all around working on ch in same manner.
7th and 8th Rows. Work even in s c.
9th Row. Increase in every 4th s c. Work 3 more rows of s c increasing a sufficient number of times in each row to keep work flat, break yarn.
THUMB: With Yellow follow directions given for thumb on page 5.
Sew the 2 sections together having the thumb to right and leaving 2 Yellow petals free at lower edge. With Green cover a bone ring with s c and sew to top of holder. ✿

SUNFLOWER *(continued from page 16)*

and fasten as before. **ROW 5**—Turn, join Orange, sc in one puff st, (2 sc in next sc, sc in next puff st) repeated around (48 sc). **ROW 6**—Repeat Row 4 (24 puffs). **ROW 7**—Turn, join Orange, ch 1, (sc in next 3 sc, 2 sc in next sc) repeated around (60 sc). Join and fasten as before. **ROW 8**—Repeat Row 4 (30 puffs). **ROW 9**—Turn, join Orange, ch 1, sc in each st around. Join and fasten as before. **ROW 10**—Repeat Row 4—(30 puffs). Fasten off Brown. **ROW 11—Petals**—With wrong-side-up, join Orange to sc between any 2 puffs, ch 7, sk 1 ch, sc in next ch, hdc in next ch, dc in next 3 ch, a 2-dc Cluster in next ch, sk next puff st, sl st in next sc. * Ch 1, turn and working in back lps only, sk sl st, sc in next 4 dc. Ch 3, turn, sk 1 ch, sc in next ch, hdc in next ch, dc in back lps of next 3 sc, a 2-dc Cluster in next sc, sk puff st, sl st in next sc. Repeat from * around (30 petals). End with sc-row and sew to 1st row.

Cover Orange center (Row 1) with Brown French Knots. Cover a bone ring with sc in Orange. Sew to one petal. Steam and press holder dry on back thru a cloth. Line back with cloth.

PENGUIN *(continued from page 27)*

3rd rnd: * 2 sc in next sc, sc in next sc. Repeat from * around. Break off.

PUPIL . . . Using a single strand of Black and No. 7 hook, work as for Eye until 2 rnds have been completed. Break off. Sew Pupil to Eye, then Eye to Head. Sew Head to Body.

BEAK . . . Using a double strand of Canary Yellow and No. 4 hook, ch 7. **1st row:** Sc in 2nd ch from hook and in each ch across. Ch 1, turn. **2nd row:** Sc in each sc across. Ch 1, turn. **3rd row:** Dec 1 sc, sc in next 2 sc, dec 1 sc. Ch 1, turn. **4th and 5th rows:** Repeat 2nd row. **6th row:** Dec 2 sc. **7th row:** Dec 1 sc. Break off. Sew Beak in place.

FOOT (Make 2) . . . Using a double strand of Canary Yellow and No. 4 hook, ch 4. **1st row:** 2 dc in 4th ch from hook. Ch 3, turn. **2nd row:** 2 dc in first dc, 3 dc in next dc, 3 dc in top of starting chain. Ch 3, turn. **3rd row:** Dc in first dc, (dc in next 2 dc, 2 dc in next dc) twice; dc in next dc, dc in top of turning chain. Ch 4, turn. **4th row:** Dc in first dc, (half dc in next dc, dc in next dc, tr in next dc, dc in next dc) twice; half dc in next dc, dc in next dc, tr in top of turning chain. Break off. Embroider webbing on Feet with Dk. Yellow. Sew Feet in place.

BOW TIE . . . Using a single strand of Black and No. 7 hook, ch 12. **1st row:** Sc in 2nd ch from hook, sc in each ch across. Ch 1, turn. **2nd to 5th rows incl:** Dec 1 sc, sc in each sc across to within last 2 sc, dec 1 sc. Ch 1, turn. **6th row:** 2 sc in first sc, sc in next sc, 2 sc in last sc. Ch 1, turn. **7th and 8th rows:** Sc in each sc across. Ch 1, turn. **9th row:** Dec 1 sc, sc in next sc, dec 1 sc. Ch 1, turn. **10th row:** Repeat 6th row. **11th, 12th and 13th rows:** 2 sc in first sc, sc in each sc across, 2 sc in last sc. Ch 1, turn. **14th row:** Repeat 7th row. Break off. Sew in place.

BUTTON (Make 3) . . . Using a single strand of Black and No. 7 hook, ch 2. **1st rnd:** 7 sc in 2nd ch from hook. Break off. Sew in place.

BACK . . . Work as for Front, using double strand of Black for entire body and omitting eye, flipper, bow tie and buttons. Do not embroider feet.

For Padding, see page 2.

Sew Front and Back pieces together. With Black sc closely around bone ring. Sew to top.

ORANGE *(continued from page 7)*

hdc in next ch, dc in next 2 ch, tr in next 2 ch, holding back the last lp of each dc on hook, make 2 dc in next ch, thread over and draw thru all lps on hook (cluster made). Sk 1 sc on ring, sl st in next sc. Repeat from * 4 times. Fasten off. Cover center with Lt. Yellow Fench Knots. Make 3 Flowers.

LEAF—With Shd. Greens Floss ch 26, sk 1 ch, * sc in next ch, hdc in next ch, dc in next 2 ch, tr in next 16 ch, dc in next 2 ch, hdc in next ch, sc in next ch, * 3 sc in end ch. Repeat from * to * on other side of ch. **ROW 2**—Ch 1, turn, sc in 1st st, hdc in next st, * (dc in next 2 sts, 2 dc in next st) 7 times, dc in next 2 sts, * in next st make 2 dc, ch 3, sl st in last dc for a p, and 2 dc. Repeat from * to *. Hdc in next st, sc in next st. Join and fasten off. Make three. **Stem**—With Green ch 24, sk 4 ch, dc in each remaining ch. Fasten off. Fold crosswise in center, forming a loop and sew ends tog. Sew 2 Leaves to Stem. Sew Leaves and Flowers on Orange as illustrated.

Steam and press dry on back thru a cloth. Line back with cloth.

FOUR ROSES *(continued from page 15)*

each d tr make 2 d tr in same place as thread was attached, thread over and draw through all loops on hook (cluster made), * ch 3, make a 3-tr cluster in same place, ch 3, in tip of next petal make dc, ch 3 and dc; ch 3, in tip of next petal make a 3-tr cluster, ch 3 and a 3-d tr cluster. Repeat from * around, ending with ch 3, sl st in tip of first cluster.

SECOND ROSE . . . Attach Green to tip of any petal, ch 5 and complete a d tr cluster as before, ch 1, sc in corresponding loop on First Rose, ch 1, make a 3-tr cluster in same place on Second Rose as last cluster was made, and complete as for Edging of First Rose, joining next 4 loops of Second Rose to corresponding loops of First Rose as before. Work Edging around remaining 2 Roses, joining to adjacent sides as before. Attach White to tip of a 3-d tr cluster at any free corner and work all around outer edges as follows: **1st rnd:** Ch 3, 2 dc in same place, 3 dc in each loop around, making 3 dc, ch 3 and 3 dc at tip of each corner d tr cluster, ending with 3 dc in same cluster as first 3-dc group was made, ch 3, sl st to 3rd ch of ch-3. Break off. **2nd rnd:** Attach Green to corner loop, ch 1, 3 sc in same loop, sc in each dc around, making 5 sc in each corner loop, and ending with 2 sc in loop where first 3 sc were made, sl st to first sc. Break off. **3rd rnd:** Attach White where sl st was made and ch 3, dc in each sc around, making dc, ch 3 and dc in center sc of each 5-sc group, and ending with dc in same place as starting ch-3, ch 3, sl st to 3rd ch of ch-3. Break off. **4th rnd:** Attach Rose and work as for 2nd rnd. Break off. **5th rnd:** Attach White and work as for 3rd rnd. Break off. **6th rnd:** Attach Yellow and work as for 2nd rnd. Break off. **7th rnd:** Attach White and work as for 3rd rnd. Break off. This completes Front piece.

BACK PIECE (Make 2) . . . Using 2 strands of White, make a chain 12 inches long. **1st row:** Sc in 2nd ch from hook and sc in each ch across until row measures 9¼ inches. (There are 65 sc in row.) Cut off remaining chain. Now sc in each sc across, decreasing 1 sc at both ends of each row until all sts are worked off, making ch 1 and turning at end of each row—*to dec 1 sc, work off 2 sc as 1 sc.* Pin the 2 Back Pieces to wrong side of Front Piece, having diagonal opening at center back.

EDGING . . . With Front facing, attach Red to any corner and, working through both thicknesses, make ch 3, 9 dc in same place as thread was attached (shell made), * skip 3 dc, sc between last dc skipped and the following dc, skip 3 dc, make 6 dc (shell) between last dc skipped and the following dc. Repeat from * around, making a 10-dc shell at corners and ending with sc, skip 3 dc, sl st to 3rd ch of starting ch-3. Break off. Pad if desired. For Padding, see page 2.